The Bible Reading Journal Series:
120 Days in the Bible.

"Your Word is a lamp to my feet.
And a light to my path."
Psalm 119:105

This Journal Belongs to:

_____

The Bible Reading Journal Series: 120 Days in the Bible.

"Again, the kingdom of heaven is like a merchant seeking fine pearls, and upon finding one pearl of great value, he went and sold all that he had and bought it."

Matthew 13:45-46

Copyright © 2019 Adriana Morales-Spokane
All rights reserved.

ISBN: 9781077210417

Scripture quotations taken from the **New American Standard Bible** © (NASB), Copyright © 1960, 1962, 1963, 1968, 1971, 1972, 1973, 1975, 1977, 1995 by The Lockman Foundation. Used by permission. www.Lockman.org

The Bible Reading Journal Series: 120 Days in the Bible.

DEDICATION

Abba Father,

You are a lighthouse in the midst of my distress. Your loving presence settles the rhythms of the open sea. Your promise is a fresh sea breeze to my soul. Your Word is an anchor to both mind and heart. Your Holy Spirit teaches me 'how to' navigate the journey. Your Wisdom helps me adjust the sails along the way.

Let us scuba dive and explore the treasures of the seas. The beauty of vivid coral reefs is awe-inspiring. You are the captain of all life adventures; I will never be lost again! You are a warm-hearted Father whose love never changes or ends.

You hear every beat of my heart!

Open your arms 'wide-open' and hold me close to your heart. Don't ever let me go. Thank you, Jesus, for being the sunrise of my troubled days. No troubles, disasters or tragedies in life will separate me from your bountiful love.

> **"nor height, nor depth, nor any other created thing, will be able to separate us from the love of God, which is in Christ Jesus our Lord."**
> **Romans 8:39**

Your forever travel companion, in Jesus' name,

I boldly praise, Amen.

Your Beloved Child.

The Bible Reading Journal Series: 120 Days in the Bible.

Welcome!

This Bible journal is a companion for your Bible Readings.

It will help you reflect and pray over selected Scriptures whether you are sitting at a kitchen table, taking a lunch break, waiting in line to pick-up your child from school or drinking a cup of coffee at a local cafe. This journal will provide you with ample journaling space to record your personal reflections when you read Bible passages for one hundred twenty days.

You will find brief, written prompts that will guide you thru spiritual disciplines: Obedience, repentance, forgiveness, thanksgiving, and prayer. This portable journal is perfect for anyone who tends to be busy throughout the day or travels often.

Adriana appreciates the journaling process. She renews her mind with His Word, strengthens her heart with His promises and refreshes her soul with His unfailing love and faithfulness.

Are you ready to establish these disciplines in your life? If so, your life will be transformed over the course of time. May the Holy Spirit be your best Counselor. I pray you rest in Jesus Christ and be refreshed in the next one hundred twenty days.

The Bible Reading Journal Series: 120 Days in the Bible.

Standing on Firm Grounds Today!

"Therefore, everyone who hears these words of Mine and acts on them, may be compared to a wise man who built his house on the rock. And the rain fell, and the floods came, and the winds blew and slammed against that house; and yet it did not fall, for it had been founded on the rock. Everyone who hears these words of Mine and does not act on them, will be like a foolish man who built his house on the sand. The rain fell, and the floods came, and the winds blew and slammed against that house; and it fell-and great was its fall." Matthew 7:24-27

Several years ago, I was standing on sinking ground with my Faith walk. Church attendance was 'hit or miss', bible reading was inconsistent, and prayerful life was non-existent. I was distant from the Lord. I was consumed by 'cultural busyness' and distracted by a fast-paced lifestyle. No margin for rest, adequate self-care or time for His Word.

Yes! You heard me right. I was standing on shaky territory.

I was a reckless woman who did not read or act on His Word. I was vulnerable and helpless. "Enemies of the heart" took root in my soul from paralyzing fear, doubt, hatred, unforgiveness, isolation to bitterness. I was resting at the bottom of the pit, 'darkness of depression', in the midst of loss and separation, and overwhelming life circumstances. I was grief-stricken with dad's sudden death, overwhelmed by a regional leadership platform and troubled by mom's relocation back to South America.

My world had drastically turned upside down in less than three months.

But God ...

He has never left me nor forsaken me.

When the Holy Spirit convicted me of His faithfulness, I immediately turned back to His Word one day at a time. Re-building an intimate relationship with the Lord was a gradual process yet it was worth the time and commitment.

Spiritual disciplines; Obedience, repentance, forgiveness, thanksgiving, and prayer transformed my life one day at a time.

He is my Refuge, Comforter and the Best Counselor. He is my Rock today. The more I read and apply His Word to my everyday life, the closer I am to the Lord. His faithfulness, favor, and grace are evident, and His mercies never run out.

I am standing on a firm foundation today.

"You shall walk in all the way which the LORD your God has commanded you, that you may live and that it may be well with you, and that you may prolong your days in the land which you will possess." Deuteronomy 5:33

"by loving the LORD your God, by obeying His voice, and by holding fast to Him; for this is your life and the length of your days, that you may live in the land which the LORD swore to

your fathers, to Abraham, Isaac, and Jacob, to give them.""
Deuteronomy 30:20

"The LORD is my rock and my fortress and my deliverer, My God, my rock, in whom I take refuge; My shield and the horn of my salvation, my stronghold."
Psalms 18:2

How to use this Journal?

This journal will assist you in recording your thoughts, reflections, and observations when reading your Bible passages. You may either be taking notes at Bible Study class, listening to a sermon in Church, at a conference, or even reading your Bible quietly in your home.

This journal will keep a record of 'how' the Lord speaks to you when actively engaged in His Word. It does not give you a specific Bible passage. It is an open forum for you to select the passages you would like to meditate on or even the ones you want to memorize over the course of one hundred twenty days. You will record your journaling experiences from the Bible.

This journal gives you an opportunity to inscribe or write the Scripture(s). When writing verses, you will engage another one of your senses, touch. Research has proven that if you use more than one of your senses in any given activity, the impact will be greater and you will be able to remember the information for longer periods of time.

I don't know about you my friend, but I experience great difficulties in memorizing His Word. Repetition has helped me over the years to hide His Truth in my heart (Proverbs 3:3). Practical application of His Word is critical in our daily walk with Jesus Christ. As a matter of fact, His Truth reminds us of the following, "For if anyone is a hearer of the word and not a doer, he is like a man who looks at his natural face in a mirror; for once he has looked at himself and gone away, he has immediately forgotten what kind of person he was. But one who looks intently at the perfect laws, the law of liberty, and abides by it, not having become a forgetful hearer but an effectual doer, this man will be blessed in what he does." (James 1: 23-25).

Testimonies

"I am so encouraged when I pray for wisdom, strength and courage! I feel so much closer to God when I pray." ~ *Rob S.*

"My relationship with God is a growing priority in my life. I cannot walk, know, and experience his glorious presence, transforming power, unending love, and awesome grace without reading the Bible daily, praying at all times, confessing my sins and faults and giving thanks for everything. Building these disciplines helps me to focus on Jesus and his kingdom, to grow in my Christian faith, to become more mature, and to be more like Jesus." ~ *Angelica L.*

"Investing your time in God's Word and seeking His Will by prayer will reveal His Glorious Promises and Faithfulness." ~ *Charissa C.*

The Bible Reading Journal Series: 120 Days in the Bible.

"Journaling has not only been therapeutic over the years but it has made a difference in my walk with Jesus. Thanksgiving has renewed my mind, Prayer has strengthened my heart and soul, and Obedience has transformed my life! There is power in the Cross." ~ *Adriana M.*

PRAYER

Heavenly Father,

You are our Lord and Savior. You died at the Cross, forgave those who sinned against you, and resurrected on the third day to offer us eternal life,

You are a Light to those who are blind-folded by temptations and a compass to those who are sleepless in the wilderness. You march closely with the broken-hearted, heal the wounds from past misfortunes, and revive our souls from shattered dreams,

You relentlessly maneuver the heights of steep mountains and execute magnificent, prized miracles in our ordinary lives!

You are a beacon in the midst of chaos and the matchless hope for today's helpless world,

You are worthy of praise, Abba Father (Psalm 145:3). Your generous hand is filled with promises and your heart sings distinct melodies of joy and hope, I'm telling the world about all the phenomenal acts you do every day.

You are an amazing God!

Your never-ending grace, unfailing love, and unmerited favor to all generations are the manifestation of your deep love for us. I want to witness your immeasurable greatness, power and strength in my life today and always.

Since your 'heart tunes' are my song of joy and hope (Psalms 59:16), I'm asking for you to always be my refuge and fortress until my last breath on earth!

In Jesus' name, I boldly pray. Amen

The Bible Reading Journal Series: 120 Days in the Bible.

**"Open my eyes, that I may behold
Wonderful things from Your law."**
Psalm 119:18

D Date: _____

S Selected Bible Passage:
_____
_____

R Reflections or Observations:
_____
_____
_____

I Inscribe the Selected Verse(s) in a different translation:
_____
_____
_____
_____
_____
_____

But He said, "On the contrary, blessed are those who hear the word of God and observe it." Luke 11:28

Lord, help me step out in obedience today…
_____
_____

"But a man must examine himself, and in so doing he is to eat of the bread and drink of the cup."
1 Corinthians 11:28

Lord, I would like to share and repent…
_____
_____

"For if you forgive others for their transgressions, your heavenly Father will also forgive you." Matthew 6:14

Lord, I need to forgive…
_____

The Bible Reading Journal Series: 120 Days in the Bible.

**"O taste and see that the LORD is good;
How blessed is the man who takes refuge in Him!"** Psalm 34:8

Lord, I praise You for today's blessings...

"Ask, and it will be given to you; seek, and you will find; knock, and it will be opened to you." Matthew 7:7

Lord, hear my prayers …

Additional Scriptures:

Other Notes:

The Bible Reading Journal Series: 120 Days in the Bible.

> **"Open my eyes, that I may behold Wonderful things from Your law."**
> Psalm 119:18

D

Date: _____

S

Selected Bible Passage:
_____
_____
_____

R

Reflections or Observations:
_____
_____
_____

I

Inscribe the Selected Verse(s) in a different translation:
_____
_____
_____
_____
_____
_____
_____

But He said, "On the contrary, blessed are those who hear the word of God and observe it." Luke 11:28

Lord, help me step out in obedience today…
_____
_____

"But a man must examine himself, and in so doing he is to eat of the bread and drink of the cup."
1 Corinthians 11:28

Lord, I would like to share and repent…
_____
_____

"For if you forgive others for their transgressions, your heavenly Father will also forgive you." Matthew 6:14

Lord, I need to forgive…
_____

**"O taste and see that the LORD is good;
How blessed is the man who takes refuge in Him!"** Psalm 34:8

Lord, I praise You for today's blessings...

"Ask, and it will be given to you; seek, and you will find; knock, and it will be opened to you." Matthew 7:7

Lord, hear my prayers …

Additional Scriptures:

Other Notes:

The Bible Reading Journal Series: 120 Days in the Bible.

**"Open my eyes, that I may behold
Wonderful things from Your law."**
Psalm 119:18

D

Date: _____

S

Selected Bible Passage:
_____
_____
_____

R

Reflections or Observations:
_____
_____
_____

I

Inscribe the Selected Verse(s) in a different translation:
_____
_____
_____
_____
_____
_____
_____

But He said, "On the contrary, blessed are those who hear the word of God and observe it." Luke 11:28

Lord, help me step out in obedience today…
_____
_____

"But a man must examine himself, and in so doing he is to eat of the bread and drink of the cup."
1 Corinthians 11:28

Lord, I would like to share and repent…
_____
_____

"For if you forgive others for their transgressions, your heavenly Father will also forgive you." Matthew 6:14

Lord, I need to forgive…
_____

The Bible Reading Journal Series: 120 Days in the Bible.

**"O taste and see that the LORD is good;
How blessed is the man who takes refuge in Him!"** Psalm 34:8

Lord, I praise You for today's blessings...

"Ask, and it will be given to you; seek, and you will find; knock, and it will be opened to you." Matthew 7:7

Lord, hear my prayers …

Additional Scriptures:

Other Notes:

The Bible Reading Journal Series: 120 Days in the Bible.

**"Open my eyes, that I may behold
Wonderful things from Your law."**
Psalm 119:18

D

Date: _____

S

Selected Bible Passage:
_____
_____
_____

R

Reflections or Observations:
_____
_____
_____

I

Inscribe the Selected Verse(s) in a different translation:
_____
_____
_____
_____
_____
_____
_____

But He said, "On the contrary, blessed are those who hear the word of God and observe it." Luke 11:28

Lord, help me step out in obedience today…
_____
_____

"But a man must examine himself, and in so doing he is to eat of the bread and drink of the cup."
1 Corinthians 11:28

Lord, I would like to share and repent…
_____
_____

"For if you forgive others for their transgressions, your heavenly Father will also forgive you." Matthew 6:14

Lord, I need to forgive…
_____

The Bible Reading Journal Series: 120 Days in the Bible.

**"O taste and see that the LORD is good;
How blessed is the man who takes refuge in Him!"** Psalm 34:8

Lord, I praise You for today's blessings...

"Ask, and it will be given to you; seek, and you will find; knock, and it will be opened to you." Matthew 7:7

Lord, hear my prayers …

Additional Scriptures:

Other Notes:

The Bible Reading Journal Series: 120 Days in the Bible.

**"Open my eyes, that I may behold
Wonderful things from Your law."**
Psalm 119:18

D   Date: _____

S   Selected Bible Passage:
_____
_____

R   Reflections or Observations:
_____
_____

I   Inscribe the Selected Verse(s) in a different translation:
_____
_____
_____
_____
_____
_____

But He said, "On the contrary, blessed are those who hear the word of God and observe it." Luke 11:28

Lord, help me step out in obedience today…
_____
_____

"But a man must examine himself, and in so doing he is to eat of the bread and drink of the cup."
1 Corinthians 11:28

Lord, I would like to share and repent…
_____
_____

"For if you forgive others for their transgressions, your heavenly Father will also forgive you." Matthew 6:14

Lord, I need to forgive…
_____

The Bible Reading Journal Series: 120 Days in the Bible.

**"O taste and see that the Lord is good;
How blessed is the man who takes refuge in Him!"** Psalm 34:8

Lord, I praise You for today's blessings...

"Ask, and it will be given to you; seek, and you will find; knock, and it will be opened to you." Matthew 7:7

Lord, hear my prayers …

Additional Scriptures:

Other Notes:

The Bible Reading Journal Series: 120 Days in the Bible.

**"Open my eyes, that I may behold
Wonderful things from Your law."**
Psalm 119:18

D Date: _____

S Selected Bible Passage:
_____
_____

R Reflections or Observations:
_____
_____
_____

I Inscribe the Selected Verse(s) in a different translation:
_____
_____
_____
_____
_____
_____

But He said, "On the contrary, blessed are those who hear the word of God and observe it." Luke 11:28

Lord, help me step out in obedience today…
_____
_____

"But a man must examine himself, and in so doing he is to eat of the bread and drink of the cup."
1 Corinthians 11:28

Lord, I would like to share and repent…
_____
_____

"For if you forgive others for their transgressions, your heavenly Father will also forgive you." Matthew 6:14

Lord, I need to forgive…
_____

The Bible Reading Journal Series: 120 Days in the Bible.

**"O taste and see that the LORD is good;
How blessed is the man who takes refuge in Him!"** Psalm 34:8

Lord, I praise You for today's blessings...

"Ask, and it will be given to you; seek, and you will find; knock, and it will be opened to you." Matthew 7:7

Lord, hear my prayers …

Additional Scriptures:

Other Notes:

The Bible Reading Journal Series: 120 Days in the Bible.

**"Open my eyes, that I may behold
Wonderful things from Your law."**
Psalm 119:18

D

Date: _____

S

Selected Bible Passage:
_____
_____
_____

R

Reflections or Observations:
_____
_____
_____

I

Inscribe the Selected Verse(s) in a different translation:
_____
_____
_____
_____
_____
_____
_____

But He said, "On the contrary, blessed are those who hear the word of God and observe it." Luke 11:28

Lord, help me step out in obedience today…
_____
_____

"But a man must examine himself, and in so doing he is to eat of the bread and drink of the cup."
1 Corinthians 11:28

Lord, I would like to share and repent…
_____
_____

"For if you forgive others for their transgressions, your heavenly Father will also forgive you." Matthew 6:14

Lord, I need to forgive…
_____

> **"O taste and see that the LORD is good;
> How blessed is the man who takes refuge in Him!"** Psalm 34:8

Lord, I praise You for today's blessings...

> **"Ask, and it will be given to you; seek, and you will find; knock, and it will be opened to you."** Matthew 7:7

Lord, hear my prayers …

Additional Scriptures:

Other Notes:

The Bible Reading Journal Series: 120 Days in the Bible.

**"Open my eyes, that I may behold
Wonderful things from Your law."**
Psalm 119:18

D Date: _____

S Selected Bible Passage:
_____
_____

R Reflections or Observations:
_____
_____

I Inscribe the Selected Verse(s) in a different translation:
_____
_____
_____
_____
_____
_____

But He said, "On the contrary, blessed are those who hear the word of God and observe it." Luke 11:28

Lord, help me step out in obedience today…
_____
_____

"But a man must examine himself, and in so doing he is to eat of the bread and drink of the cup."
1 Corinthians 11:28

Lord, I would like to share and repent…
_____
_____

"For if you forgive others for their transgressions, your heavenly Father will also forgive you." Matthew 6:14

Lord, I need to forgive…
_____

**"O taste and see that the LORD is good;
How blessed is the man who takes refuge in Him!"** Psalm 34:8

Lord, I praise You for today's blessings...

"Ask, and it will be given to you; seek, and you will find; knock, and it will be opened to you." Matthew 7:7

Lord, hear my prayers …

Additional Scriptures:

Other Notes:

The Bible Reading Journal Series: 120 Days in the Bible.

**"Open my eyes, that I may behold
Wonderful things from Your law."**
Psalm 119:18

D

Date: _____

S

Selected Bible Passage:
_____
_____
_____

R

Reflections or Observations:
_____
_____
_____

I

Inscribe the Selected Verse(s) in a different translation:
_____
_____
_____
_____
_____
_____
_____

But He said, "On the contrary, blessed are those who hear the word of God and observe it." Luke 11:28

Lord, help me step out in obedience today…
_____
_____

"But a man must examine himself, and in so doing he is to eat of the bread and drink of the cup."
1 Corinthians 11:28

Lord, I would like to share and repent…
_____
_____

"For if you forgive others for their transgressions, your heavenly Father will also forgive you." Matthew 6:14

Lord, I need to forgive…
_____

The Bible Reading Journal Series: 120 Days in the Bible.

**"O taste and see that the LORD is good;
How blessed is the man who takes refuge in Him!"** Psalm 34:8

Lord, I praise You for today's blessings...

"Ask, and it will be given to you; seek, and you will find; knock, and it will be opened to you." Matthew 7:7

Lord, hear my prayers …

Additional Scriptures:

Other Notes:

The Bible Reading Journal Series: 120 Days in the Bible.

**"Open my eyes, that I may behold
Wonderful things from Your law."**
Psalm 119:18

D

Date: _____

S

Selected Bible Passage:
_____
_____
_____

R

Reflections or Observations:
_____
_____
_____

I

Inscribe the Selected Verse(s) in a different translation:
_____
_____
_____
_____
_____
_____
_____

But He said, "On the contrary, blessed are those who hear the word of God and observe it." Luke 11:28

Lord, help me step out in obedience today…
_____
_____

"But a man must examine himself, and in so doing he is to eat of the bread and drink of the cup."
1 Corinthians 11:28

Lord, I would like to share and repent…
_____
_____

"For if you forgive others for their transgressions, your heavenly Father will also forgive you." Matthew 6:14

Lord, I need to forgive…
_____

The Bible Reading Journal Series: 120 Days in the Bible.

**"O taste and see that the LORD is good;
How blessed is the man who takes refuge in Him!"** Psalm 34:8

Lord, I praise You for today's blessings...

"Ask, and it will be given to you; seek, and you will find; knock, and it will be opened to you." Matthew 7:7

Lord, hear my prayers …

Additional Scriptures:

Other Notes:

The Bible Reading Journal Series: 120 Days in the Bible.

**"Open my eyes, that I may behold
Wonderful things from Your law."**
Psalm 119:18

D

Date: _____

S

Selected Bible Passage:
_____
_____
_____

R

Reflections or Observations:
_____
_____
_____

I

Inscribe the Selected Verse(s) in a different translation:
_____
_____
_____
_____
_____
_____
_____

But He said, "On the contrary, blessed are those who hear the word of God and observe it." Luke 11:28

Lord, help me step out in obedience today…
_____
_____

"But a man must examine himself, and in so doing he is to eat of the bread and drink of the cup."
1 Corinthians 11:28

Lord, I would like to share and repent…
_____
_____

"For if you forgive others for their transgressions, your heavenly Father will also forgive you." Matthew 6:14

Lord, I need to forgive…
_____

The Bible Reading Journal Series: 120 Days in the Bible.

"O taste and see that the LORD **is good;**
How blessed is the man who takes refuge in Him!" Psalm 34:8

Lord, I praise You for today's blessings...

_____
_____

"Ask, and it will be given to you; seek, and you will find; knock, and it will be opened to you." Matthew 7:7

Lord, hear my prayers …

_____
_____
_____
_____

Additional Scriptures:

_____
_____
_____
_____
_____
_____
_____
_____
_____

Other Notes:

_____
_____
_____
_____
_____
_____
_____
_____
_____
_____
_____
_____
_____
_____
_____
_____
_____
_____
_____

The Bible Reading Journal Series: 120 Days in the Bible.

**"Open my eyes, that I may behold
Wonderful things from Your law."**
Psalm 119:18

D

Date: _____

S

Selected Bible Passage:
_____
_____
_____

R

Reflections or Observations:
_____
_____
_____

I

Inscribe the Selected Verse(s) in a different translation:
_____
_____
_____
_____
_____
_____
_____

But He said, "On the contrary, blessed are those who hear the word of God and observe it." Luke 11:28

Lord, help me step out in obedience today…
_____
_____

"But a man must examine himself, and in so doing he is to eat of the bread and drink of the cup."
1 Corinthians 11:28

Lord, I would like to share and repent…
_____
_____

"For if you forgive others for their transgressions, your heavenly Father will also forgive you." Matthew 6:14

Lord, I need to forgive…
_____

**"O taste and see that the LORD is good;
How blessed is the man who takes refuge in Him!"** Psalm 34:8

Lord, I praise You for today's blessings...

"Ask, and it will be given to you; seek, and you will find; knock, and it will be opened to you." Matthew 7:7

Lord, hear my prayers …

Additional Scriptures:

Other Notes:

The Bible Reading Journal Series: 120 Days in the Bible.

**"Open my eyes, that I may behold
Wonderful things from Your law."**
Psalm 119:18

D

Date: _____

S

Selected Bible Passage:
_____
_____

R

Reflections or Observations:
_____
_____
_____

I

Inscribe the Selected Verse(s) in a different translation:
_____
_____
_____
_____
_____
_____

But He said, "On the contrary, blessed are those who hear the word of God and observe it." Luke 11:28

Lord, help me step out in obedience today…
_____
_____

"But a man must examine himself, and in so doing he is to eat of the bread and drink of the cup."
1 Corinthians 11:28

Lord, I would like to share and repent…
_____
_____

"For if you forgive others for their transgressions, your heavenly Father will also forgive you." Matthew 6:14

Lord, I need to forgive…
_____

The Bible Reading Journal Series: 120 Days in the Bible.

**"O taste and see that the Lord is good;
How blessed is the man who takes refuge in Him!"** Psalm 34:8

Lord, I praise You for today's blessings...

"Ask, and it will be given to you; seek, and you will find; knock, and it will be opened to you." Matthew 7:7

Lord, hear my prayers ...

Additional Scriptures:

Other Notes:

The Bible Reading Journal Series: 120 Days in the Bible.

**"Open my eyes, that I may behold
Wonderful things from Your law."**
Psalm 119:18

D

Date: _____

S

Selected Bible Passage:
_____
_____

R

Reflections or Observations:
_____
_____
_____

I

Inscribe the Selected Verse(s) in a different translation:
_____
_____
_____
_____
_____
_____
_____

But He said, "On the contrary, blessed are those who hear the word of God and observe it." Luke 11:28

Lord, help me step out in obedience today…
_____
_____

"But a man must examine himself, and in so doing he is to eat of the bread and drink of the cup."
1 Corinthians 11:28

Lord, I would like to share and repent…
_____
_____

"For if you forgive others for their transgressions, your heavenly Father will also forgive you." Matthew 6:14

Lord, I need to forgive…
_____

The Bible Reading Journal Series: 120 Days in the Bible.

**"O taste and see that the LORD is good;
How blessed is the man who takes refuge in Him!"** Psalm 34:8

Lord, I praise You for today's blessings...

"Ask, and it will be given to you; seek, and you will find; knock, and it will be opened to you." Matthew 7:7

Lord, hear my prayers …

Additional Scriptures:

Other Notes:

The Bible Reading Journal Series: 120 Days in the Bible.

**"Open my eyes, that I may behold
Wonderful things from Your law."**
Psalm 119:18

D Date: _____

S Selected Bible Passage:
_____
_____
_____

R Reflections or Observations:
_____
_____
_____

I Inscribe the Selected Verse(s) in a different translation:
_____
_____
_____
_____
_____
_____
_____

But He said, "On the contrary, blessed are those who hear the word of God and observe it." Luke 11:28

Lord, help me step out in obedience today…
_____
_____

"But a man must examine himself, and in so doing he is to eat of the bread and drink of the cup."
1 Corinthians 11:28

Lord, I would like to share and repent…
_____
_____

"For if you forgive others for their transgressions, your heavenly Father will also forgive you." Matthew 6:14

Lord, I need to forgive…
_____

**"O taste and see that the LORD is good;
How blessed is the man who takes refuge in Him!"** Psalm 34:8

Lord, I praise You for today's blessings...

"Ask, and it will be given to you; seek, and you will find; knock, and it will be opened to you." Matthew 7:7

Lord, hear my prayers …

Additional Scriptures:

Other Notes:

The Bible Reading Journal Series: 120 Days in the Bible.

**"Open my eyes, that I may behold
Wonderful things from Your law."**
Psalm 119:18

D Date: _____

S Selected Bible Passage:
_____
_____

R Reflections or Observations:
_____
_____
_____

I Inscribe the Selected Verse(s) in a different translation:
_____
_____
_____
_____
_____
_____
_____

But He said, "On the contrary, blessed are those who hear the word of God and observe it." Luke 11:28

Lord, help me step out in obedience today…
_____
_____

"But a man must examine himself, and in so doing he is to eat of the bread and drink of the cup."
1 Corinthians 11:28

Lord, I would like to share and repent…
_____
_____

"For if you forgive others for their transgressions, your heavenly Father will also forgive you." Matthew 6:14

Lord, I need to forgive…
_____

The Bible Reading Journal Series: 120 Days in the Bible.

**"O taste and see that the LORD is good;
How blessed is the man who takes refuge in Him!"** Psalm 34:8

Lord, I praise You for today's blessings...

"Ask, and it will be given to you; seek, and you will find; knock, and it will be opened to you." Matthew 7:7

Lord, hear my prayers …

Additional Scriptures:

Other Notes:

The Bible Reading Journal Series: 120 Days in the Bible.

**"Open my eyes, that I may behold
Wonderful things from Your law."**
Psalm 119:18

D Date: _____

S Selected Bible Passage:
_____
_____

R Reflections or Observations:
_____
_____

I Inscribe the Selected Verse(s) in a different translation:
_____
_____
_____
_____
_____
_____
_____

But He said, "On the contrary, blessed are those who hear the word of God and observe it." Luke 11:28

Lord, help me step out in obedience today…
_____
_____

"But a man must examine himself, and in so doing he is to eat of the bread and drink of the cup."
1 Corinthians 11:28

Lord, I would like to share and repent…
_____
_____

"For if you forgive others for their transgressions, your heavenly Father will also forgive you." Matthew 6:14

Lord, I need to forgive…
_____

> **"O taste and see that the LORD is good;**
> **How blessed is the man who takes refuge in Him!"** Psalm 34:8

Lord, I praise You for today's blessings...

_____
_____

> **"Ask, and it will be given to you; seek, and you will find; knock, and it will be opened to you."** Matthew 7:7

Lord, hear my prayers …

_____
_____
_____
_____

Additional Scriptures:

_____
_____
_____
_____
_____
_____
_____
_____
_____
_____

Other Notes:

_____
_____
_____
_____
_____
_____
_____
_____
_____
_____
_____
_____
_____
_____
_____
_____
_____
_____
_____

The Bible Reading Journal Series: 120 Days in the Bible.

**"Open my eyes, that I may behold
Wonderful things from Your law."**
Psalm 119:18

D   Date: _____

S   Selected Bible Passage:
_____
_____

R   Reflections or Observations:
_____
_____
_____

I   Inscribe the Selected Verse(s) in a different translation:
_____
_____
_____
_____
_____
_____

But He said, "On the contrary, blessed are those who hear the word of God and observe it." Luke 11:28

Lord, help me step out in obedience today…
_____
_____

"But a man must examine himself, and in so doing he is to eat of the bread and drink of the cup."
1 Corinthians 11:28

Lord, I would like to share and repent…
_____
_____

"For if you forgive others for their transgressions, your heavenly Father will also forgive you." Matthew 6:14

Lord, I need to forgive…
_____

The Bible Reading Journal Series: 120 Days in the Bible.

**"O taste and see that the LORD is good;
How blessed is the man who takes refuge in Him!"** Psalm 34:8

Lord, I praise You for today's blessings...

"Ask, and it will be given to you; seek, and you will find; knock, and it will be opened to you." Matthew 7:7

Lord, hear my prayers …

Additional Scriptures:

Other Notes:

The Bible Reading Journal Series: 120 Days in the Bible.

**"Open my eyes, that I may behold
Wonderful things from Your law."**
Psalm 119:18

D Date: _____

S Selected Bible Passage:
_____
_____

R Reflections or Observations:
_____
_____

I Inscribe the Selected Verse(s) in a different translation:
_____
_____
_____
_____
_____
_____
_____

But He said, "On the contrary, blessed are those who hear the word of God and observe it." Luke 11:28

Lord, help me step out in obedience today…
_____
_____

"But a man must examine himself, and in so doing he is to eat of the bread and drink of the cup."
1 Corinthians 11:28

Lord, I would like to share and repent…
_____
_____

"For if you forgive others for their transgressions, your heavenly Father will also forgive you." Matthew 6:14

Lord, I need to forgive…
_____

The Bible Reading Journal Series: 120 Days in the Bible.

**"O taste and see that the Lord is good;
How blessed is the man who takes refuge in Him!"** Psalm 34:8

Lord, I praise You for today's blessings...

"Ask, and it will be given to you; seek, and you will find; knock, and it will be opened to you." Matthew 7:7

Lord, hear my prayers …

Additional Scriptures:

Other Notes:

The Bible Reading Journal Series: 120 Days in the Bible.

**"Open my eyes, that I may behold
Wonderful things from Your law."**
Psalm 119:18

D

Date: _____

S

Selected Bible Passage:
_____
_____

R

Reflections or Observations:
_____
_____

I

Inscribe the Selected Verse(s) in a different translation:
_____
_____
_____
_____
_____
_____

But He said, "On the contrary, blessed are those who hear the word of God and observe it." Luke 11:28

Lord, help me step out in obedience today…
_____
_____

"But a man must examine himself, and in so doing he is to eat of the bread and drink of the cup."
1 Corinthians 11:28

Lord, I would like to share and repent…
_____
_____

"For if you forgive others for their transgressions, your heavenly Father will also forgive you." Matthew 6:14

Lord, I need to forgive…
_____

The Bible Reading Journal Series: 120 Days in the Bible.

**"O taste and see that the LORD is good;
How blessed is the man who takes refuge in Him!"** Psalm 34:8

Lord, I praise You for today's blessings...
_____
_____

"Ask, and it will be given to you; seek, and you will find; knock, and it will be opened to you." Matthew 7:7

Lord, hear my prayers …
_____
_____
_____
_____

Additional Scriptures:
_____
_____
_____
_____
_____
_____
_____
_____
_____
_____

Other Notes:
_____
_____
_____
_____
_____
_____
_____
_____
_____
_____
_____
_____
_____
_____
_____
_____
_____
_____
_____
_____

The Bible Reading Journal Series: 120 Days in the Bible.

**"Open my eyes, that I may behold
Wonderful things from Your law."**
Psalm 119:18

D

Date: _____

S

Selected Bible Passage:
_____
_____
_____

R

Reflections or Observations:
_____
_____
_____

I

Inscribe the Selected Verse(s) in a different translation:
_____
_____
_____
_____
_____
_____
_____

But He said, "On the contrary, blessed are those who hear the word of God and observe it." Luke 11:28

Lord, help me step out in obedience today…
_____
_____

"But a man must examine himself, and in so doing he is to eat of the bread and drink of the cup."
1 Corinthians 11:28

Lord, I would like to share and repent…
_____
_____

"For if you forgive others for their transgressions, your heavenly Father will also forgive you." Matthew 6:14

Lord, I need to forgive…
_____

The Bible Reading Journal Series: 120 Days in the Bible.

**"O taste and see that the LORD is good;
How blessed is the man who takes refuge in Him!"** Psalm 34:8

Lord, I praise You for today's blessings...

"Ask, and it will be given to you; seek, and you will find; knock, and it will be opened to you." Matthew 7:7

Lord, hear my prayers …

Additional Scriptures:

Other Notes:

The Bible Reading Journal Series: 120 Days in the Bible.

**"Open my eyes, that I may behold
Wonderful things from Your law."**
Psalm 119:18

D

Date: _____

S

Selected Bible Passage:
_____
_____
_____

R

Reflections or Observations:
_____
_____
_____

I

Inscribe the Selected Verse(s) in a different translation:
_____
_____
_____
_____
_____
_____
_____

But He said, "On the contrary, blessed are those who hear the word of God and observe it." Luke 11:28

Lord, help me step out in obedience today…
_____
_____

"But a man must examine himself, and in so doing he is to eat of the bread and drink of the cup."
1 Corinthians 11:28

Lord, I would like to share and repent…
_____
_____

"For if you forgive others for their transgressions, your heavenly Father will also forgive you." Matthew 6:14

Lord, I need to forgive…
_____

The Bible Reading Journal Series: 120 Days in the Bible.

"O taste and see that the LORD **is good;
How blessed is the man who takes refuge in Him!"** Psalm 34:8

Lord, I praise You for today's blessings...

"Ask, and it will be given to you; seek, and you will find; knock, and it will be opened to you." Matthew 7:7

Lord, hear my prayers …

Additional Scriptures:

Other Notes:

The Bible Reading Journal Series: 120 Days in the Bible.

**"Open my eyes, that I may behold
Wonderful things from Your law."**
Psalm 119:18

D

Date: _____

S

Selected Bible Passage:
_____
_____

R

Reflections or Observations:
_____
_____
_____

I

Inscribe the Selected Verse(s) in a different translation:
_____
_____
_____
_____
_____
_____
_____

But He said, "On the contrary, blessed are those who hear the word of God and observe it." Luke 11:28

Lord, help me step out in obedience today…
_____
_____

"But a man must examine himself, and in so doing he is to eat of the bread and drink of the cup."
1 Corinthians 11:28

Lord, I would like to share and repent…
_____
_____

"For if you forgive others for their transgressions, your heavenly Father will also forgive you." Matthew 6:14

Lord, I need to forgive…
_____

The Bible Reading Journal Series: 120 Days in the Bible.

**"O taste and see that the Lord is good;
How blessed is the man who takes refuge in Him!"** Psalm 34:8

Lord, I praise You for today's blessings...

_____
_____

"Ask, and it will be given to you; seek, and you will find; knock, and it will be opened to you." Matthew 7:7

Lord, hear my prayers …

_____
_____
_____
_____

Additional Scriptures:

_____
_____
_____
_____
_____
_____
_____
_____
_____
_____

Other Notes:

_____
_____
_____
_____
_____
_____
_____
_____
_____
_____
_____
_____
_____
_____
_____
_____
_____
_____
_____

The Bible Reading Journal Series: 120 Days in the Bible.

> **"Open my eyes, that I may behold
> Wonderful things from Your law."**
> Psalm 119:18

D

Date: _____

S

Selected Bible Passage:
_____
_____
_____

R

Reflections or Observations:
_____
_____
_____

I

Inscribe the Selected Verse(s) in a different translation:
_____
_____
_____
_____
_____
_____
_____

But He said, "On the contrary, blessed are those who hear the word of God and observe it." Luke 11:28

Lord, help me step out in obedience today…
_____
_____

"But a man must examine himself, and in so doing he is to eat of the bread and drink of the cup."
1 Corinthians 11:28

Lord, I would like to share and repent…
_____
_____

"For if you forgive others for their transgressions, your heavenly Father will also forgive you." Matthew 6:14

Lord, I need to forgive…
_____

**"O taste and see that the LORD is good;
How blessed is the man who takes refuge in Him!"** Psalm 34:8

Lord, I praise You for today's blessings...

"Ask, and it will be given to you; seek, and you will find; knock, and it will be opened to you." Matthew 7:7

Lord, hear my prayers …

Additional Scriptures:

Other Notes:

The Bible Reading Journal Series: 120 Days in the Bible.

**"Open my eyes, that I may behold
Wonderful things from Your law."**
Psalm 119:18

D

Date: _____

S

Selected Bible Passage:

_____
_____
_____

R

Reflections or Observations:

_____
_____
_____

I

Inscribe the Selected Verse(s) in a different translation:

_____
_____
_____
_____
_____
_____
_____
_____

But He said, "On the contrary, blessed are those who hear the word of God and observe it." Luke 11:28

Lord, help me step out in obedience today…
_____
_____

"But a man must examine himself, and in so doing he is to eat of the bread and drink of the cup."
1 Corinthians 11:28

Lord, I would like to share and repent…
_____
_____

"For if you forgive others for their transgressions, your heavenly Father will also forgive you." Matthew 6:14

Lord, I need to forgive…
_____

The Bible Reading Journal Series: 120 Days in the Bible.

**"O taste and see that the LORD is good;
How blessed is the man who takes refuge in Him!"** Psalm 34:8

Lord, I praise You for today's blessings...

"Ask, and it will be given to you; seek, and you will find; knock, and it will be opened to you." Matthew 7:7

Lord, hear my prayers …

Additional Scriptures:

Other Notes:

The Bible Reading Journal Series: 120 Days in the Bible.

**"Open my eyes, that I may behold
Wonderful things from Your law."**
Psalm 119:18

D
Date: _____

S
Selected Bible Passage:
_____
_____

R
Reflections or Observations:
_____
_____

I
Inscribe the Selected Verse(s) in a different translation:
_____
_____
_____
_____
_____
_____

But He said, "On the contrary, blessed are those who hear the word of God and observe it." Luke 11:28

Lord, help me step out in obedience today…
_____
_____

"But a man must examine himself, and in so doing he is to eat of the bread and drink of the cup."
1 Corinthians 11:28

Lord, I would like to share and repent…
_____
_____

"For if you forgive others for their transgressions, your heavenly Father will also forgive you." Matthew 6:14

Lord, I need to forgive…
_____

The Bible Reading Journal Series: 120 Days in the Bible.

**"O taste and see that the LORD is good;
How blessed is the man who takes refuge in Him!"** Psalm 34:8

Lord, I praise You for today's blessings...

"Ask, and it will be given to you; seek, and you will find; knock, and it will be opened to you." Matthew 7:7

Lord, hear my prayers …

Additional Scriptures:

Other Notes:

The Bible Reading Journal Series: 120 Days in the Bible.

**"Open my eyes, that I may behold
Wonderful things from Your law."**
Psalm 119:18

D

Date: _____

S

Selected Bible Passage:
_____
_____
_____

R

Reflections or Observations:
_____
_____
_____

I

Inscribe the Selected Verse(s) in a different translation:
_____
_____
_____
_____
_____
_____
_____

But He said, "On the contrary, blessed are those who hear the word of God and observe it." Luke 11:28

Lord, help me step out in obedience today…
_____
_____

"But a man must examine himself, and in so doing he is to eat of the bread and drink of the cup."
1 Corinthians 11:28

Lord, I would like to share and repent…
_____
_____

"For if you forgive others for their transgressions, your heavenly Father will also forgive you." Matthew 6:14

Lord, I need to forgive…
_____

**"O taste and see that the LORD is good;
How blessed is the man who takes refuge in Him!"** Psalm 34:8

Lord, I praise You for today's blessings...

"Ask, and it will be given to you; seek, and you will find; knock, and it will be opened to you." Matthew 7:7

Lord, hear my prayers …

Additional Scriptures:

Other Notes:

The Bible Reading Journal Series: 120 Days in the Bible.

**"Open my eyes, that I may behold
Wonderful things from Your law."**
Psalm 119:18

D Date: _____

S Selected Bible Passage:
_____
_____

R Reflections or Observations:
_____
_____

I Inscribe the Selected Verse(s) in a different translation:
_____
_____
_____
_____
_____
_____

But He said, "On the contrary, blessed are those who hear the word of God and observe it." Luke 11:28

Lord, help me step out in obedience today…
_____
_____

"But a man must examine himself, and in so doing he is to eat of the bread and drink of the cup."
1 Corinthians 11:28

Lord, I would like to share and repent…
_____
_____

"For if you forgive others for their transgressions, your heavenly Father will also forgive you." Matthew 6:14

Lord, I need to forgive…
_____

**"O taste and see that the LORD is good;
How blessed is the man who takes refuge in Him!"** Psalm 34:8

Lord, I praise You for today's blessings...

"Ask, and it will be given to you; seek, and you will find; knock, and it will be opened to you." Matthew 7:7

Lord, hear my prayers …

Additional Scriptures:

Other Notes:

The Bible Reading Journal Series: 120 Days in the Bible.

**"Open my eyes, that I may behold
Wonderful things from Your law."**
Psalm 119:18

D

Date: _____

S

Selected Bible Passage:
_____
_____
_____

R

Reflections or Observations:
_____
_____
_____

I

Inscribe the Selected Verse(s) in a different translation:
_____
_____
_____
_____
_____
_____
_____

But He said, "On the contrary, blessed are those who hear the word of God and observe it." Luke 11:28

Lord, help me step out in obedience today…
_____
_____

"But a man must examine himself, and in so doing he is to eat of the bread and drink of the cup."
1 Corinthians 11:28

Lord, I would like to share and repent…
_____
_____

"For if you forgive others for their transgressions, your heavenly Father will also forgive you." Matthew 6:14

Lord, I need to forgive…
_____

The Bible Reading Journal Series: 120 Days in the Bible.

**"O taste and see that the LORD is good;
How blessed is the man who takes refuge in Him!"** Psalm 34:8

Lord, I praise You for today's blessings...

"Ask, and it will be given to you; seek, and you will find; knock, and it will be opened to you." Matthew 7:7

Lord, hear my prayers …

Additional Scriptures:

Other Notes:

The Bible Reading Journal Series: 120 Days in the Bible.

**"Open my eyes, that I may behold
Wonderful things from Your law."**
Psalm 119:18

D

Date: _____

S

Selected Bible Passage:
_____
_____
_____

R

Reflections or Observations:
_____
_____
_____

I

Inscribe the Selected Verse(s) in a different translation:
_____
_____
_____
_____
_____
_____

But He said, "On the contrary, blessed are those who hear the word of God and observe it." Luke 11:28

Lord, help me step out in obedience today…
_____
_____

"But a man must examine himself, and in so doing he is to eat of the bread and drink of the cup."
1 Corinthians 11:28

Lord, I would like to share and repent…
_____
_____

"For if you forgive others for their transgressions, your heavenly Father will also forgive you." Matthew 6:14

Lord, I need to forgive…
_____

**"O taste and see that the LORD is good;
How blessed is the man who takes refuge in Him!"** Psalm 34:8

Lord, I praise You for today's blessings...

"Ask, and it will be given to you; seek, and you will find; knock, and it will be opened to you." Matthew 7:7

Lord, hear my prayers …

Additional Scriptures:

Other Notes:

The Bible Reading Journal Series: 120 Days in the Bible.

**"Open my eyes, that I may behold
Wonderful things from Your law."**
Psalm 119:18

D

Date: _____

S

Selected Bible Passage:
_____
_____

R

Reflections or Observations:
_____
_____

I

Inscribe the Selected Verse(s) in a different translation:
_____
_____
_____
_____
_____
_____
_____

But He said, "On the contrary, blessed are those who hear the word of God and observe it." Luke 11:28

Lord, help me step out in obedience today...
_____
_____

"But a man must examine himself, and in so doing he is to eat of the bread and drink of the cup."
1 Corinthians 11:28

Lord, I would like to share and repent...
_____
_____

"For if you forgive others for their transgressions, your heavenly Father will also forgive you." Matthew 6:14

Lord, I need to forgive...
_____

The Bible Reading Journal Series: 120 Days in the Bible.

"O taste and see that the Lord is good;
How blessed is the man who takes refuge in Him!" Psalm 34:8

Lord, I praise You for today's blessings...

"Ask, and it will be given to you; seek, and you will find; knock, and it will be opened to you." Matthew 7:7

Lord, hear my prayers …

Additional Scriptures:

Other Notes:

The Bible Reading Journal Series: 120 Days in the Bible.

**"Open my eyes, that I may behold
Wonderful things from Your law."**
Psalm 119:18

D Date: _____

S Selected Bible Passage:
_____
_____
_____

R Reflections or Observations:
_____
_____
_____

I Inscribe the Selected Verse(s) in a different translation:
_____
_____
_____
_____
_____
_____
_____

But He said, "On the contrary, blessed are those who hear the word of God and observe it." Luke 11:28

Lord, help me step out in obedience today…
_____
_____

"But a man must examine himself, and in so doing he is to eat of the bread and drink of the cup."
1 Corinthians 11:28

Lord, I would like to share and repent…
_____
_____

"For if you forgive others for their transgressions, your heavenly Father will also forgive you." Matthew 6:14

Lord, I need to forgive…
_____

The Bible Reading Journal Series: 120 Days in the Bible.

**"O taste and see that the LORD is good;
How blessed is the man who takes refuge in Him!"** Psalm 34:8

Lord, I praise You for today's blessings...

"Ask, and it will be given to you; seek, and you will find; knock, and it will be opened to you." Matthew 7:7

Lord, hear my prayers …

Additional Scriptures:

Other Notes:

The Bible Reading Journal Series: 120 Days in the Bible.

**"Open my eyes, that I may behold
Wonderful things from Your law."**
Psalm 119:18

D

Date: _____

S

Selected Bible Passage:
_____
_____
_____

R

Reflections or Observations:
_____
_____
_____

I

Inscribe the Selected Verse(s) in a different translation:
_____
_____
_____
_____
_____
_____
_____

But He said, "On the contrary, blessed are those who hear the word of God and observe it." Luke 11:28

Lord, help me step out in obedience today…
_____
_____

"But a man must examine himself, and in so doing he is to eat of the bread and drink of the cup."
1 Corinthians 11:28

Lord, I would like to share and repent…
_____
_____

"For if you forgive others for their transgressions, your heavenly Father will also forgive you." Matthew 6:14

Lord, I need to forgive…
_____

The Bible Reading Journal Series: 120 Days in the Bible.

**"O taste and see that the LORD is good;
How blessed is the man who takes refuge in Him!"** Psalm 34:8

Lord, I praise You for today's blessings...

"Ask, and it will be given to you; seek, and you will find; knock, and it will be opened to you." Matthew 7:7

Lord, hear my prayers …

Additional Scriptures:

Other Notes:

The Bible Reading Journal Series: 120 Days in the Bible.

**"Open my eyes, that I may behold
Wonderful things from Your law."**
Psalm 119:18

D

Date: _____

S

Selected Bible Passage:
_____
_____
_____

R

Reflections or Observations:
_____
_____
_____

I

Inscribe the Selected Verse(s) in a different translation:
_____
_____
_____
_____
_____
_____
_____

But He said, "On the contrary, blessed are those who hear the word of God and observe it." Luke 11:28

Lord, help me step out in obedience today…
_____
_____

"But a man must examine himself, and in so doing he is to eat of the bread and drink of the cup."
1 Corinthians 11:28

Lord, I would like to share and repent…
_____
_____

"For if you forgive others for their transgressions, your heavenly Father will also forgive you." Matthew 6:14

Lord, I need to forgive…
_____

The Bible Reading Journal Series: 120 Days in the Bible.

**"O taste and see that the LORD is good;
How blessed is the man who takes refuge in Him!"** Psalm 34:8

Lord, I praise You for today's blessings...

"Ask, and it will be given to you; seek, and you will find; knock, and it will be opened to you." Matthew 7:7

Lord, hear my prayers …

Additional Scriptures:

Other Notes:

The Bible Reading Journal Series: 120 Days in the Bible.

**"Open my eyes, that I may behold
Wonderful things from Your law."**
Psalm 119:18

D Date: _____

S Selected Bible Passage:
_____
_____
_____

R Reflections or Observations:
_____
_____
_____

I Inscribe the Selected Verse(s) in a different translation:
_____
_____
_____
_____
_____
_____
_____

But He said, "On the contrary, blessed are those who hear the word of God and observe it." Luke 11:28

Lord, help me step out in obedience today…
_____
_____

"But a man must examine himself, and in so doing he is to eat of the bread and drink of the cup."
1 Corinthians 11:28

Lord, I would like to share and repent…
_____
_____

"For if you forgive others for their transgressions, your heavenly Father will also forgive you." Matthew 6:14

Lord, I need to forgive…
_____

The Bible Reading Journal Series: 120 Days in the Bible.

"O taste and see that the LORD **is good;**
How blessed is the man who takes refuge in Him!" Psalm 34:8

Lord, I praise You for today's blessings...

"Ask, and it will be given to you; seek, and you will find; knock, and it will be opened to you." Matthew 7:7

Lord, hear my prayers …

Additional Scriptures:

Other Notes:

The Bible Reading Journal Series: 120 Days in the Bible.

**"Open my eyes, that I may behold
Wonderful things from Your law."**
Psalm 119:18

D

Date: _____

S

Selected Bible Passage:
_____
_____
_____

R

Reflections or Observations:
_____
_____
_____

I

Inscribe the Selected Verse(s) in a different translation:
_____
_____
_____
_____
_____
_____
_____

But He said, "On the contrary, blessed are those who hear the word of God and observe it." Luke 11:28

Lord, help me step out in obedience today…
_____
_____

"But a man must examine himself, and in so doing he is to eat of the bread and drink of the cup."
1 Corinthians 11:28

Lord, I would like to share and repent…
_____
_____

"For if you forgive others for their transgressions, your heavenly Father will also forgive you." Matthew 6:14

Lord, I need to forgive…
_____

The Bible Reading Journal Series: 120 Days in the Bible.

**"O taste and see that the LORD is good;
How blessed is the man who takes refuge in Him!"** Psalm 34:8

Lord, I praise You for today's blessings...

"Ask, and it will be given to you; seek, and you will find; knock, and it will be opened to you." Matthew 7:7

Lord, hear my prayers …

Additional Scriptures:

Other Notes:

The Bible Reading Journal Series: 120 Days in the Bible.

**"Open my eyes, that I may behold
Wonderful things from Your law."**
Psalm 119:18

D

Date: _____

S

Selected Bible Passage:
_____
_____
_____

R

Reflections or Observations:
_____
_____
_____

I

Inscribe the Selected Verse(s) in a different translation:
_____
_____
_____
_____
_____
_____
_____

But He said, "On the contrary, blessed are those who hear the word of God and observe it." Luke 11:28

Lord, help me step out in obedience today…
_____
_____

"But a man must examine himself, and in so doing he is to eat of the bread and drink of the cup."
1 Corinthians 11:28

Lord, I would like to share and repent…
_____
_____

"For if you forgive others for their transgressions, your heavenly Father will also forgive you." Matthew 6:14

Lord, I need to forgive…
_____

**"O taste and see that the LORD is good;
How blessed is the man who takes refuge in Him!"** Psalm 34:8

Lord, I praise You for today's blessings...

"Ask, and it will be given to you; seek, and you will find; knock, and it will be opened to you." Matthew 7:7

Lord, hear my prayers …

Additional Scriptures:

Other Notes:

The Bible Reading Journal Series: 120 Days in the Bible.

**"Open my eyes, that I may behold
Wonderful things from Your law."**
. Psalm 119:18

D Date: _____

S Selected Bible Passage:
_____
_____

R Reflections or Observations:
_____
_____
_____

I Inscribe the Selected Verse(s) in a different translation:
_____
_____
_____
_____
_____
_____

But He said, "On the contrary, blessed are those who hear the word of God and observe it." Luke 11:28

Lord, help me step out in obedience today...
_____
_____

"But a man must examine himself, and in so doing he is to eat of the bread and drink of the cup."
1 Corinthians 11:28

Lord, I would like to share and repent...
_____
_____

"For if you forgive others for their transgressions, your heavenly Father will also forgive you." Matthew 6:14

Lord, I need to forgive...
_____

The Bible Reading Journal Series: 120 Days in the Bible.

**"O taste and see that the LORD is good;
How blessed is the man who takes refuge in Him!"** Psalm 34:8

Lord, I praise You for today's blessings...

"Ask, and it will be given to you; seek, and you will find; knock, and it will be opened to you." Matthew 7:7

Lord, hear my prayers …

Additional Scriptures:

Other Notes:

The Bible Reading Journal Series: 120 Days in the Bible.

**"Open my eyes, that I may behold
Wonderful things from Your law."**
Psalm 119:18

D Date: _____

S Selected Bible Passage:
_____
_____
_____

R Reflections or Observations:
_____
_____
_____

I Inscribe the Selected Verse(s) in a different translation:
_____
_____
_____
_____
_____
_____
_____

But He said, "On the contrary, blessed are those who hear the word of God and observe it." Luke 11:28

Lord, help me step out in obedience today…
_____
_____

"But a man must examine himself, and in so doing he is to eat of the bread and drink of the cup."
1 Corinthians 11:28

Lord, I would like to share and repent…
_____
_____

"For if you forgive others for their transgressions, your heavenly Father will also forgive you." Matthew 6:14

Lord, I need to forgive…
_____

**"O taste and see that the LORD is good;
How blessed is the man who takes refuge in Him!"** Psalm 34:8

Lord, I praise You for today's blessings...

"Ask, and it will be given to you; seek, and you will find; knock, and it will be opened to you." Matthew 7:7

Lord, hear my prayers …

Additional Scriptures:

Other Notes:

The Bible Reading Journal Series: 120 Days in the Bible.

**"Open my eyes, that I may behold
Wonderful things from Your law."**
Psalm 119:18

D

Date: _____

S

Selected Bible Passage:
_____
_____
_____

R

Reflections or Observations:
_____
_____
_____

I

Inscribe the Selected Verse(s) in a different translation:
_____
_____
_____
_____
_____
_____
_____

But He said, "On the contrary, blessed are those who hear the word of God and observe it." Luke 11:28

Lord, help me step out in obedience today…
_____
_____

"But a man must examine himself, and in so doing he is to eat of the bread and drink of the cup."
1 Corinthians 11:28

Lord, I would like to share and repent…
_____
_____

"For if you forgive others for their transgressions, your heavenly Father will also forgive you." Matthew 6:14

Lord, I need to forgive…
_____

**"O taste and see that the LORD is good;
How blessed is the man who takes refuge in Him!"** Psalm 34:8

Lord, I praise You for today's blessings...

"Ask, and it will be given to you; seek, and you will find; knock, and it will be opened to you." Matthew 7:7

Lord, hear my prayers …

Additional Scriptures:

Other Notes:

The Bible Reading Journal Series: 120 Days in the Bible.

**"Open my eyes, that I may behold
Wonderful things from Your law."**
Psalm 119:18

D Date: _____

S Selected Bible Passage:
_____
_____
_____

R Reflections or Observations:
_____
_____
_____

I Inscribe the Selected Verse(s) in a different translation:
_____
_____
_____
_____
_____
_____
_____

But He said, "On the contrary, blessed are those who hear the word of God and observe it." Luke 11:28

Lord, help me step out in obedience today…
_____
_____

"But a man must examine himself, and in so doing he is to eat of the bread and drink of the cup."
1 Corinthians 11:28

Lord, I would like to share and repent…
_____
_____

"For if you forgive others for their transgressions, your heavenly Father will also forgive you." Matthew 6:14

Lord, I need to forgive…
_____

The Bible Reading Journal Series: 120 Days in the Bible.

**"O taste and see that the LORD is good;
How blessed is the man who takes refuge in Him!"** Psalm 34:8

Lord, I praise You for today's blessings...

"Ask, and it will be given to you; seek, and you will find; knock, and it will be opened to you." Matthew 7:7

Lord, hear my prayers …

Additional Scriptures:

Other Notes:

The Bible Reading Journal Series: 120 Days in the Bible.

**"Open my eyes, that I may behold
Wonderful things from Your law."**
Psalm 119:18

D

Date: _____

S

Selected Bible Passage:
_____
_____

R

Reflections or Observations:
_____
_____

I

Inscribe the Selected Verse(s) in a different translation:
_____
_____
_____
_____
_____
_____
_____

But He said, "On the contrary, blessed are those who hear the word of God and observe it." Luke 11:28

Lord, help me step out in obedience today…
_____
_____

"But a man must examine himself, and in so doing he is to eat of the bread and drink of the cup."
1 Corinthians 11:28

Lord, I would like to share and repent…
_____
_____

"For if you forgive others for their transgressions, your heavenly Father will also forgive you." Matthew 6:14

Lord, I need to forgive…
_____

The Bible Reading Journal Series: 120 Days in the Bible.

**"O taste and see that the LORD is good;
How blessed is the man who takes refuge in Him!"** Psalm 34:8

Lord, I praise You for today's blessings...

"Ask, and it will be given to you; seek, and you will find; knock, and it will be opened to you." Matthew 7:7

Lord, hear my prayers …

Additional Scriptures:

Other Notes:

The Bible Reading Journal Series: 120 Days in the Bible.

**"Open my eyes, that I may behold
Wonderful things from Your law."**
Psalm 119:18

D Date: _____

S Selected Bible Passage:
_____
_____

R Reflections or Observations:
_____
_____
_____

I Inscribe the Selected Verse(s) in a different translation:
_____
_____
_____
_____
_____
_____
_____

But He said, "On the contrary, blessed are those who hear the word of God and observe it." Luke 11:28

Lord, help me step out in obedience today…
_____
_____

"But a man must examine himself, and in so doing he is to eat of the bread and drink of the cup."
1 Corinthians 11:28

Lord, I would like to share and repent…
_____
_____

"For if you forgive others for their transgressions, your heavenly Father will also forgive you." Matthew 6:14

Lord, I need to forgive…
_____

The Bible Reading Journal Series: 120 Days in the Bible.

**"O taste and see that the Lord is good;
How blessed is the man who takes refuge in Him!"** Psalm 34:8

Lord, I praise You for today's blessings...

"Ask, and it will be given to you; seek, and you will find; knock, and it will be opened to you." Matthew 7:7

Lord, hear my prayers …

Additional Scriptures:

Other Notes:

The Bible Reading Journal Series: 120 Days in the Bible.

**"Open my eyes, that I may behold
Wonderful things from Your law."**
Psalm 119:18

D

Date: _____

S

Selected Bible Passage:
_____
_____
_____

R

Reflections or Observations:
_____
_____
_____

I

Inscribe the Selected Verse(s) in a different translation:
_____
_____
_____
_____
_____
_____
_____

But He said, "On the contrary, blessed are those who hear the word of God and observe it." Luke 11:28

Lord, help me step out in obedience today…
_____
_____

"But a man must examine himself, and in so doing he is to eat of the bread and drink of the cup."
1 Corinthians 11:28

Lord, I would like to share and repent…
_____
_____

"For if you forgive others for their transgressions, your heavenly Father will also forgive you." Matthew 6:14

Lord, I need to forgive…
_____

**"O taste and see that the LORD is good;
How blessed is the man who takes refuge in Him!"** Psalm 34:8

Lord, I praise You for today's blessings...

"Ask, and it will be given to you; seek, and you will find; knock, and it will be opened to you." Matthew 7:7

Lord, hear my prayers …

Additional Scriptures:

Other Notes:

The Bible Reading Journal Series: 120 Days in the Bible.

**"Open my eyes, that I may behold
Wonderful things from Your law."**
Psalm 119:18

D Date: _____

S Selected Bible Passage:
_____
_____

R Reflections or Observations:
_____
_____
_____

I Inscribe the Selected Verse(s) in a different translation:
_____
_____
_____
_____
_____
_____
_____

But He said, "On the contrary, blessed are those who hear the word of God and observe it." Luke 11:28

Lord, help me step out in obedience today…
_____
_____

"But a man must examine himself, and in so doing he is to eat of the bread and drink of the cup."
1 Corinthians 11:28

Lord, I would like to share and repent…
_____
_____

"For if you forgive others for their transgressions, your heavenly Father will also forgive you." Matthew 6:14

Lord, I need to forgive…
_____

The Bible Reading Journal Series: 120 Days in the Bible.

"O taste and see that the LORD **is good;**
How blessed is the man who takes refuge in Him!" Psalm 34:8

Lord, I praise You for today's blessings...

"Ask, and it will be given to you; seek, and you will find; knock, and it will be opened to you." Matthew 7:7

Lord, hear my prayers …

Additional Scriptures:

Other Notes:

The Bible Reading Journal Series: 120 Days in the Bible.

**"Open my eyes, that I may behold
Wonderful things from Your law."**
Psalm 119:18

D

Date: _____

S

Selected Bible Passage:
_____
_____
_____

R

Reflections or Observations:
_____
_____
_____

I

Inscribe the Selected Verse(s) in a different translation:
_____
_____
_____
_____
_____
_____
_____

But He said, "On the contrary, blessed are those who hear the word of God and observe it." Luke 11:28

Lord, help me step out in obedience today…
_____
_____

"But a man must examine himself, and in so doing he is to eat of the bread and drink of the cup."
1 Corinthians 11:28

Lord, I would like to share and repent…
_____
_____

"For if you forgive others for their transgressions, your heavenly Father will also forgive you." Matthew 6:14

Lord, I need to forgive…
_____

The Bible Reading Journal Series: 120 Days in the Bible.

"O taste and see that the LORD **is good;**
How blessed is the man who takes refuge in Him!" Psalm 34:8

Lord, I praise You for today's blessings...

"Ask, and it will be given to you; seek, and you will find; knock, and it will be opened to you." Matthew 7:7

Lord, hear my prayers …

Additional Scriptures:

Other Notes:

The Bible Reading Journal Series: 120 Days in the Bible.

**"Open my eyes, that I may behold
Wonderful things from Your law."**
Psalm 119:18

D

Date: _____

S

Selected Bible Passage:
_____
_____

R

Reflections or Observations:
_____
_____

I

Inscribe the Selected Verse(s) in a different translation:
_____
_____
_____
_____
_____
_____
_____

But He said, "On the contrary, blessed are those who hear the word of God and observe it." Luke 11:28

Lord, help me step out in obedience today…
_____
_____

"But a man must examine himself, and in so doing he is to eat of the bread and drink of the cup."
1 Corinthians 11:28

Lord, I would like to share and repent…
_____
_____

"For if you forgive others for their transgressions, your heavenly Father will also forgive you." Matthew 6:14

Lord, I need to forgive…
_____

The Bible Reading Journal Series: 120 Days in the Bible.

**"O taste and see that the LORD is good;
How blessed is the man who takes refuge in Him!"** Psalm 34:8

Lord, I praise You for today's blessings...

"Ask, and it will be given to you; seek, and you will find; knock, and it will be opened to you." Matthew 7:7

Lord, hear my prayers …

Additional Scriptures:

Other Notes:

The Bible Reading Journal Series: 120 Days in the Bible.

**"Open my eyes, that I may behold
Wonderful things from Your law."**
Psalm 119:18

D

Date: _____

S

Selected Bible Passage:
_____
_____
_____

R

Reflections or Observations:
_____
_____
_____

I

Inscribe the Selected Verse(s) in a different translation:
_____
_____
_____
_____
_____
_____
_____

But He said, "On the contrary, blessed are those who hear the word of God and observe it." Luke 11:28

Lord, help me step out in obedience today…
_____
_____

"But a man must examine himself, and in so doing he is to eat of the bread and drink of the cup."
1 Corinthians 11:28

Lord, I would like to share and repent…
_____
_____

"For if you forgive others for their transgressions, your heavenly Father will also forgive you." Matthew 6:14

Lord, I need to forgive…
_____

The Bible Reading Journal Series: 120 Days in the Bible.

"O taste and see that the L**ord**** is good;
How blessed is the man who takes refuge in Him!"** Psalm 34:8

Lord, I praise You for today's blessings...

"Ask, and it will be given to you; seek, and you will find; knock, and it will be opened to you." Matthew 7:7

Lord, hear my prayers …

Additional Scriptures:

Other Notes:

The Bible Reading Journal Series: 120 Days in the Bible.

**"Open my eyes, that I may behold
Wonderful things from Your law."**
Psalm 119:18

D

Date: _____

S

Selected Bible Passage:
_____
_____
_____

R

Reflections or Observations:
_____
_____
_____

I

Inscribe the Selected Verse(s) in a different translation:
_____
_____
_____
_____
_____
_____

But He said, "On the contrary, blessed are those who hear the word of God and observe it." Luke 11:28

Lord, help me step out in obedience today…
_____
_____

"But a man must examine himself, and in so doing he is to eat of the bread and drink of the cup."
1 Corinthians 11:28

Lord, I would like to share and repent…
_____
_____

"For if you forgive others for their transgressions, your heavenly Father will also forgive you." Matthew 6:14

Lord, I need to forgive…
_____
_____

The Bible Reading Journal Series: 120 Days in the Bible.

"O taste and see that the LORD **is good;
How blessed is the man who takes refuge in Him!"** Psalm 34:8

Lord, I praise You for today's blessings...

"Ask, and it will be given to you; seek, and you will find; knock, and it will be opened to you." Matthew 7:7

Lord, hear my prayers …

Additional Scriptures:

Other Notes:

The Bible Reading Journal Series: 120 Days in the Bible.

**"Open my eyes, that I may behold
Wonderful things from Your law."**
Psalm 119:18

D Date: _____

S Selected Bible Passage:
_____
_____
_____

R Reflections or Observations:
_____
_____
_____

I Inscribe the Selected Verse(s) in a different translation:
_____
_____
_____
_____
_____
_____
_____

But He said, "On the contrary, blessed are those who hear the word of God and observe it." Luke 11:28

Lord, help me step out in obedience today…
_____
_____

"But a man must examine himself, and in so doing he is to eat of the bread and drink of the cup."
1 Corinthians 11:28

Lord, I would like to share and repent…
_____
_____

"For if you forgive others for their transgressions, your heavenly Father will also forgive you." Matthew 6:14

Lord, I need to forgive…
_____

The Bible Reading Journal Series: 120 Days in the Bible.

> **"O taste and see that the LORD is good;**
> **How blessed is the man who takes refuge in Him!"** Psalm 34:8

Lord, I praise You for today's blessings...

"Ask, and it will be given to you; seek, and you will find; knock, and it will be opened to you." Matthew 7:7

Lord, hear my prayers …

Additional Scriptures:

Other Notes:

The Bible Reading Journal Series: 120 Days in the Bible.

**"Open my eyes, that I may behold
Wonderful things from Your law."**
Psalm 119:18

D Date: _____

S Selected Bible Passage:
_____
_____
_____

R Reflections or Observations:
_____
_____

I Inscribe the Selected Verse(s) in a different translation:
_____
_____
_____
_____
_____
_____

But He said, "On the contrary, blessed are those who hear the word of God and observe it." Luke 11:28

Lord, help me step out in obedience today…
_____
_____

"But a man must examine himself, and in so doing he is to eat of the bread and drink of the cup."
1 Corinthians 11:28

Lord, I would like to share and repent…
_____
_____

"For if you forgive others for their transgressions, your heavenly Father will also forgive you." Matthew 6:14

Lord, I need to forgive…
_____

The Bible Reading Journal Series: 120 Days in the Bible.

**"O taste and see that the LORD is good;
How blessed is the man who takes refuge in Him!"** Psalm 34:8

Lord, I praise You for today's blessings...

"Ask, and it will be given to you; seek, and you will find; knock, and it will be opened to you." Matthew 7:7

Lord, hear my prayers …

Additional Scriptures:

Other Notes:

The Bible Reading Journal Series: 120 Days in the Bible.

**"Open my eyes, that I may behold
Wonderful things from Your law."**
Psalm 119:18

D

Date: _____

S

Selected Bible Passage:
_____
_____
_____

R

Reflections or Observations:
_____
_____
_____

I

Inscribe the Selected Verse(s) in a different translation:
_____
_____
_____
_____
_____
_____
_____

But He said, "On the contrary, blessed are those who hear the word of God and observe it." Luke 11:28

Lord, help me step out in obedience today…
_____
_____

"But a man must examine himself, and in so doing he is to eat of the bread and drink of the cup."
1 Corinthians 11:28

Lord, I would like to share and repent…
_____
_____

"For if you forgive others for their transgressions, your heavenly Father will also forgive you." Matthew 6:14

Lord, I need to forgive…
_____

The Bible Reading Journal Series: 120 Days in the Bible.

**"O taste and see that the Lord is good;
How blessed is the man who takes refuge in Him!"** Psalm 34:8

Lord, I praise You for today's blessings...

___

"Ask, and it will be given to you; seek, and you will find; knock, and it will be opened to you." Matthew 7:7

Lord, hear my prayers …

___

Additional Scriptures:

___

Other Notes:

The Bible Reading Journal Series: 120 Days in the Bible.

**"Open my eyes, that I may behold
Wonderful things from Your law."**
Psalm 119:18

D Date: _____

S Selected Bible Passage:
_____
_____
_____

R Reflections or Observations:
_____
_____
_____

I Inscribe the Selected Verse(s) in a different translation:
_____
_____
_____
_____
_____
_____

But He said, "On the contrary, blessed are those who hear the word of God and observe it." Luke 11:28

Lord, help me step out in obedience today…
_____
_____

"But a man must examine himself, and in so doing he is to eat of the bread and drink of the cup."
1 Corinthians 11:28

Lord, I would like to share and repent…
_____
_____

"For if you forgive others for their transgressions, your heavenly Father will also forgive you." Matthew 6:14

Lord, I need to forgive…
_____

**"O taste and see that the LORD is good;
How blessed is the man who takes refuge in Him!"** Psalm 34:8

Lord, I praise You for today's blessings...

"Ask, and it will be given to you; seek, and you will find; knock, and it will be opened to you." Matthew 7:7

Lord, hear my prayers …

Additional Scriptures:

Other Notes:

The Bible Reading Journal Series: 120 Days in the Bible.

**"Open my eyes, that I may behold
Wonderful things from Your law."**
Psalm 119:18

D

Date: _____

S

Selected Bible Passage:
_____
_____
_____

R

Reflections or Observations:
_____
_____
_____

I

Inscribe the Selected Verse(s) in a different translation:
_____
_____
_____
_____
_____
_____

But He said, "On the contrary, blessed are those who hear the word of God and observe it." Luke 11:28

Lord, help me step out in obedience today…
_____
_____

"But a man must examine himself, and in so doing he is to eat of the bread and drink of the cup."
1 Corinthians 11:28

Lord, I would like to share and repent…
_____
_____

"For if you forgive others for their transgressions, your heavenly Father will also forgive you." Matthew 6:14

Lord, I need to forgive…
_____

The Bible Reading Journal Series: 120 Days in the Bible.

**"O taste and see that the Lord is good;
How blessed is the man who takes refuge in Him!"** Psalm 34:8

Lord, I praise You for today's blessings...

"Ask, and it will be given to you; seek, and you will find; knock, and it will be opened to you." Matthew 7:7

Lord, hear my prayers …

Additional Scriptures:

Other Notes:

The Bible Reading Journal Series: 120 Days in the Bible.

**"Open my eyes, that I may behold
Wonderful things from Your law."**
Psalm 119:18

D

Date: _____

S

Selected Bible Passage:
_____
_____
_____

R

Reflections or Observations:
_____
_____
_____

I

Inscribe the Selected Verse(s) in a different translation:
_____
_____
_____
_____
_____
_____

But He said, "On the contrary, blessed are those who hear the word of God and observe it." Luke 11:28

Lord, help me step out in obedience today…
_____
_____

"But a man must examine himself, and in so doing he is to eat of the bread and drink of the cup."
1 Corinthians 11:28

Lord, I would like to share and repent…
_____
_____

"For if you forgive others for their transgressions, your heavenly Father will also forgive you." Matthew 6:14

Lord, I need to forgive…
_____

The Bible Reading Journal Series: 120 Days in the Bible.

**"O taste and see that the LORD is good;
How blessed is the man who takes refuge in Him!"** Psalm 34:8

Lord, I praise You for today's blessings...

"Ask, and it will be given to you; seek, and you will find; knock, and it will be opened to you." Matthew 7:7

Lord, hear my prayers …

Additional Scriptures:

Other Notes:

The Bible Reading Journal Series: 120 Days in the Bible.

**"Open my eyes, that I may behold
Wonderful things from Your law."**
Psalm 119:18

D

Date: _____

S

Selected Bible Passage:
_____
_____
_____

R

Reflections or Observations:
_____
_____
_____

I

Inscribe the Selected Verse(s) in a different translation:
_____
_____
_____
_____
_____
_____
_____

But He said, "On the contrary, blessed are those who hear the word of God and observe it." Luke 11:28

Lord, help me step out in obedience today…
_____
_____

"But a man must examine himself, and in so doing he is to eat of the bread and drink of the cup."
1 Corinthians 11:28

Lord, I would like to share and repent…
_____
_____

"For if you forgive others for their transgressions, your heavenly Father will also forgive you." Matthew 6:14

Lord, I need to forgive…
_____

The Bible Reading Journal Series: 120 Days in the Bible.

**"O taste and see that the LORD is good;
How blessed is the man who takes refuge in Him!"** Psalm 34:8

Lord, I praise You for today's blessings...

"Ask, and it will be given to you; seek, and you will find; knock, and it will be opened to you." Matthew 7:7

Lord, hear my prayers …

Additional Scriptures:

Other Notes:

The Bible Reading Journal Series: 120 Days in the Bible.

**"Open my eyes, that I may behold
Wonderful things from Your law."**
Psalm 119:18

D

Date: _____

S

Selected Bible Passage:
_____
_____
_____

R

Reflections or Observations:
_____
_____
_____

I

Inscribe the Selected Verse(s) in a different translation:
_____
_____
_____
_____
_____
_____
_____

But He said, "On the contrary, blessed are those who hear the word of God and observe it." Luke 11:28

Lord, help me step out in obedience today…
_____
_____

"But a man must examine himself, and in so doing he is to eat of the bread and drink of the cup."
1 Corinthians 11:28

Lord, I would like to share and repent…
_____
_____

"For if you forgive others for their transgressions, your heavenly Father will also forgive you." Matthew 6:14

Lord, I need to forgive…
_____

The Bible Reading Journal Series: 120 Days in the Bible.

> **"O taste and see that the LORD is good;**
> **How blessed is the man who takes refuge in Him!"** Psalm 34:8

Lord, I praise You for today's blessings...

"Ask, and it will be given to you; seek, and you will find; knock, and it will be opened to you." Matthew 7:7

Lord, hear my prayers …

Additional Scriptures:

Other Notes:

The Bible Reading Journal Series: 120 Days in the Bible.

**"Open my eyes, that I may behold
Wonderful things from Your law."**
Psalm 119:18

D

Date: _____

S

Selected Bible Passage:
_____
_____
_____

R

Reflections or Observations:
_____
_____
_____

I

Inscribe the Selected Verse(s) in a different translation:
_____
_____
_____
_____
_____
_____
_____

But He said, "On the contrary, blessed are those who hear the word of God and observe it." Luke 11:28

Lord, help me step out in obedience today…
_____
_____

"But a man must examine himself, and in so doing he is to eat of the bread and drink of the cup."
1 Corinthians 11:28

Lord, I would like to share and repent…
_____
_____

"For if you forgive others for their transgressions, your heavenly Father will also forgive you." Matthew 6:14

Lord, I need to forgive…
_____

**"O taste and see that the LORD is good;
How blessed is the man who takes refuge in Him!"** Psalm 34:8

Lord, I praise You for today's blessings...

"Ask, and it will be given to you; seek, and you will find; knock, and it will be opened to you." Matthew 7:7

Lord, hear my prayers …

Additional Scriptures:

Other Notes:

The Bible Reading Journal Series: 120 Days in the Bible.

**"Open my eyes, that I may behold
Wonderful things from Your law."**
Psalm 119:18

D

Date: _____

S

Selected Bible Passage:
_____
_____
_____

R

Reflections or Observations:
_____
_____
_____

I

Inscribe the Selected Verse(s) in a different translation:
_____
_____
_____
_____
_____
_____
_____

But He said, "On the contrary, blessed are those who hear the word of God and observe it." Luke 11:28

Lord, help me step out in obedience today…
_____
_____

"But a man must examine himself, and in so doing he is to eat of the bread and drink of the cup."
1 Corinthians 11:28

Lord, I would like to share and repent…
_____
_____

"For if you forgive others for their transgressions, your heavenly Father will also forgive you." Matthew 6:14

Lord, I need to forgive…
_____

The Bible Reading Journal Series: 120 Days in the Bible.

**"O taste and see that the LORD is good;
How blessed is the man who takes refuge in Him!"** Psalm 34:8

Lord, I praise You for today's blessings...

_____
_____

"Ask, and it will be given to you; seek, and you will find; knock, and it will be opened to you." Matthew 7:7

Lord, hear my prayers …

_____
_____
_____
_____

Additional Scriptures:

_____
_____
_____
_____
_____
_____
_____
_____
_____
_____

Other Notes:

_____
_____
_____
_____
_____
_____
_____
_____
_____
_____
_____
_____
_____
_____
_____
_____
_____

The Bible Reading Journal Series: 120 Days in the Bible.

**"Open my eyes, that I may behold
Wonderful things from Your law."**
Psalm 119:18

D

Date: _____

S

Selected Bible Passage:
_____
_____
_____

R

Reflections or Observations:
_____
_____
_____

I

Inscribe the Selected Verse(s) in a different translation:
_____
_____
_____
_____
_____
_____

But He said, "On the contrary, blessed are those who hear the word of God and observe it." Luke 11:28

Lord, help me step out in obedience today…
_____
_____

"But a man must examine himself, and in so doing he is to eat of the bread and drink of the cup."
1 Corinthians 11:28

Lord, I would like to share and repent…
_____
_____

"For if you forgive others for their transgressions, your heavenly Father will also forgive you." Matthew 6:14

Lord, I need to forgive…
_____

The Bible Reading Journal Series: 120 Days in the Bible.

**"O taste and see that the LORD is good;
How blessed is the man who takes refuge in Him!"** Psalm 34:8

Lord, I praise You for today's blessings...

"Ask, and it will be given to you; seek, and you will find; knock, and it will be opened to you." Matthew 7:7

Lord, hear my prayers …

Additional Scriptures:

Other Notes:

The Bible Reading Journal Series: 120 Days in the Bible.

**"Open my eyes, that I may behold
Wonderful things from Your law."**
Psalm 119:18

D

Date: _____

S

Selected Bible Passage:
_____
_____
_____

R

Reflections or Observations:
_____
_____
_____

I

Inscribe the Selected Verse(s) in a different translation:
_____
_____
_____
_____
_____
_____

But He said, "On the contrary, blessed are those who hear the word of God and observe it." Luke 11:28

Lord, help me step out in obedience today…
_____
_____

"But a man must examine himself, and in so doing he is to eat of the bread and drink of the cup."
1 Corinthians 11:28

Lord, I would like to share and repent…
_____
_____

"For if you forgive others for their transgressions, your heavenly Father will also forgive you." Matthew 6:14

Lord, I need to forgive…
_____

The Bible Reading Journal Series: 120 Days in the Bible.

"O taste and see that the LORD **is good;
How blessed is the man who takes refuge in Him!"** Psalm 34:8

Lord, I praise You for today's blessings...

"Ask, and it will be given to you; seek, and you will find; knock, and it will be opened to you." Matthew 7:7

Lord, hear my prayers …

Additional Scriptures:

Other Notes:

The Bible Reading Journal Series: 120 Days in the Bible.

**"Open my eyes, that I may behold
Wonderful things from Your law."**
Psalm 119:18

D

Date: _____

S

Selected Bible Passage:
_____
_____
_____

R

Reflections or Observations:
_____
_____
_____

I

Inscribe the Selected Verse(s) in a different translation:
_____
_____
_____
_____
_____
_____
_____

But He said, "On the contrary, blessed are those who hear the word of God and observe it." Luke 11:28

Lord, help me step out in obedience today…
_____
_____

"But a man must examine himself, and in so doing he is to eat of the bread and drink of the cup."
1 Corinthians 11:28

Lord, I would like to share and repent…
_____
_____

"For if you forgive others for their transgressions, your heavenly Father will also forgive you." Matthew 6:14

Lord, I need to forgive…
_____

The Bible Reading Journal Series: 120 Days in the Bible.

**"O taste and see that the Lord is good;
How blessed is the man who takes refuge in Him!"** Psalm 34:8

Lord, I praise You for today's blessings...

___

"Ask, and it will be given to you; seek, and you will find; knock, and it will be opened to you." Matthew 7:7

Lord, hear my prayers ...

___

Additional Scriptures:

___

Other Notes:

___

The Bible Reading Journal Series: 120 Days in the Bible.

**"Open my eyes, that I may behold
Wonderful things from Your law."**
Psalm 119:18

D

Date: _____

S

Selected Bible Passage:
_____
_____
_____

R

Reflections or Observations:
_____
_____
_____

I

Inscribe the Selected Verse(s) in a different translation:
_____
_____
_____
_____
_____
_____
_____

But He said, "On the contrary, blessed are those who hear the word of God and observe it." Luke 11:28

Lord, help me step out in obedience today…
_____
_____

"But a man must examine himself, and in so doing he is to eat of the bread and drink of the cup."
1 Corinthians 11:28

Lord, I would like to share and repent…
_____
_____

"For if you forgive others for their transgressions, your heavenly Father will also forgive you." Matthew 6:14

Lord, I need to forgive…
_____

The Bible Reading Journal Series: 120 Days in the Bible.

**"O taste and see that the LORD is good;
How blessed is the man who takes refuge in Him!"** Psalm 34:8

Lord, I praise You for today's blessings...

"Ask, and it will be given to you; seek, and you will find; knock, and it will be opened to you." Matthew 7:7

Lord, hear my prayers …

Additional Scriptures:

Other Notes:

The Bible Reading Journal Series: 120 Days in the Bible.

**"Open my eyes, that I may behold
Wonderful things from Your law."**
Psalm 119:18

D

Date: _____

S

Selected Bible Passage:
_____
_____
_____

R

Reflections or Observations:
_____
_____
_____

I

Inscribe the Selected Verse(s) in a different translation:
_____
_____
_____
_____
_____
_____

But He said, "On the contrary, blessed are those who hear the word of God and observe it." Luke 11:28

Lord, help me step out in obedience today…
_____
_____

"But a man must examine himself, and in so doing he is to eat of the bread and drink of the cup."
1 Corinthians 11:28

Lord, I would like to share and repent…
_____
_____

"For if you forgive others for their transgressions, your heavenly Father will also forgive you." Matthew 6:14

Lord, I need to forgive…
_____

The Bible Reading Journal Series: 120 Days in the Bible.

> **"O taste and see that the LORD is good;**
> **How blessed is the man who takes refuge in Him!"** Psalm 34:8

Lord, I praise You for today's blessings...

"Ask, and it will be given to you; seek, and you will find; knock, and it will be opened to you." Matthew 7:7

Lord, hear my prayers …

Additional Scriptures:

Other Notes:

The Bible Reading Journal Series: 120 Days in the Bible.

**"Open my eyes, that I may behold
Wonderful things from Your law."**
Psalm 119:18

D

Date: _____

S

Selected Bible Passage:
_____
_____
_____

R

Reflections or Observations:
_____
_____
_____

I

Inscribe the Selected Verse(s) in a different translation:
_____
_____
_____
_____
_____
_____

But He said, "On the contrary, blessed are those who hear the word of God and observe it." Luke 11:28

Lord, help me step out in obedience today…
_____
_____

"But a man must examine himself, and in so doing he is to eat of the bread and drink of the cup."
1 Corinthians 11:28

Lord, I would like to share and repent…
_____
_____

"For if you forgive others for their transgressions, your heavenly Father will also forgive you." Matthew 6:14

Lord, I need to forgive…
_____

The Bible Reading Journal Series: 120 Days in the Bible.

**"O taste and see that the Lord is good;
How blessed is the man who takes refuge in Him!"** Psalm 34:8

Lord, I praise You for today's blessings...

"Ask, and it will be given to you; seek, and you will find; knock, and it will be opened to you." Matthew 7:7

Lord, hear my prayers …

Additional Scriptures:

Other Notes:

The Bible Reading Journal Series: 120 Days in the Bible.

**"Open my eyes, that I may behold
Wonderful things from Your law."**
Psalm 119:18

D

Date: _____

S

Selected Bible Passage:
_____
_____

R

Reflections or Observations:
_____
_____

I

Inscribe the Selected Verse(s) in a different translation:
_____
_____
_____
_____
_____

But He said, "On the contrary, blessed are those who hear the word of God and observe it." Luke 11:28

Lord, help me step out in obedience today…
_____
_____

"But a man must examine himself, and in so doing he is to eat of the bread and drink of the cup."
1 Corinthians 11:28

Lord, I would like to share and repent…
_____
_____

"For if you forgive others for their transgressions, your heavenly Father will also forgive you." Matthew 6:14

Lord, I need to forgive…
_____

> **"O taste and see that the LORD is good;
> How blessed is the man who takes refuge in Him!"** Psalm 34:8

Lord, I praise You for today's blessings...

> **"Ask, and it will be given to you; seek, and you will find; knock, and it will be opened to you."** Matthew 7:7

Lord, hear my prayers ...

Additional Scriptures:

Other Notes:

The Bible Reading Journal Series: 120 Days in the Bible.

**"Open my eyes, that I may behold
Wonderful things from Your law."**
Psalm 119:18

D

Date: _____

S

Selected Bible Passage:

___

R

Reflections or Observations:

___

I

Inscribe the Selected Verse(s) in a different translation:

___

But He said, "On the contrary, blessed are those who hear the word of God and observe it." Luke 11:28

Lord, help me step out in obedience today…

___

"But a man must examine himself, and in so doing he is to eat of the bread and drink of the cup."
1 Corinthians 11:28

Lord, I would like to share and repent…

___

"For if you forgive others for their transgressions, your heavenly Father will also forgive you." Matthew 6:14

Lord, I need to forgive…

___

The Bible Reading Journal Series: 120 Days in the Bible.

"O taste and see that the LORD **is good;**
How blessed is the man who takes refuge in Him!" Psalm 34:8

Lord, I praise You for today's blessings...

"Ask, and it will be given to you; seek, and you will find; knock, and it will be opened to you." Matthew 7:7

Lord, hear my prayers …

Additional Scriptures:

Other Notes:

The Bible Reading Journal Series: 120 Days in the Bible.

**"Open my eyes, that I may behold
Wonderful things from Your law."**
Psalm 119:18

D

Date: _____

S

Selected Bible Passage:
_____
_____
_____

R

Reflections or Observations:
_____
_____
_____

I

Inscribe the Selected Verse(s) in a different translation:
_____
_____
_____
_____
_____
_____

But He said, "On the contrary, blessed are those who hear the word of God and observe it." Luke 11:28

Lord, help me step out in obedience today…
_____
_____

"But a man must examine himself, and in so doing he is to eat of the bread and drink of the cup."
1 Corinthians 11:28

Lord, I would like to share and repent…
_____
_____

"For if you forgive others for their transgressions, your heavenly Father will also forgive you." Matthew 6:14

Lord, I need to forgive…
_____

The Bible Reading Journal Series: 120 Days in the Bible.

**"O taste and see that the LORD is good;
How blessed is the man who takes refuge in Him!"** Psalm 34:8

Lord, I praise You for today's blessings...

"Ask, and it will be given to you; seek, and you will find; knock, and it will be opened to you." Matthew 7:7

Lord, hear my prayers …

Additional Scriptures:

Other Notes:

The Bible Reading Journal Series: 120 Days in the Bible.

**"Open my eyes, that I may behold
Wonderful things from Your law."**
Psalm 119:18

D

Date: _____

S

Selected Bible Passage: _____
_____
_____

R

Reflections or Observations: _____
_____
_____

I

Inscribe the Selected Verse(s) in a different translation:
_____
_____
_____
_____
_____
_____

But He said, "On the contrary, blessed are those who hear the word of God and observe it." Luke 11:28

Lord, help me step out in obedience today…
_____
_____

"But a man must examine himself, and in so doing he is to eat of the bread and drink of the cup."
1 Corinthians 11:28

Lord, I would like to share and repent…
_____
_____

"For if you forgive others for their transgressions, your heavenly Father will also forgive you." Matthew 6:14

Lord, I need to forgive…
_____

**"O taste and see that the LORD is good;
How blessed is the man who takes refuge in Him!"** Psalm 34:8

Lord, I praise You for today's blessings...

"Ask, and it will be given to you; seek, and you will find; knock, and it will be opened to you." Matthew 7:7

Lord, hear my prayers …

Additional Scriptures:

Other Notes:

The Bible Reading Journal Series: 120 Days in the Bible.

> **"Open my eyes, that I may behold
> Wonderful things from Your law."**
> Psalm 119:18

D

Date: _____

S

Selected Bible Passage:
_____
_____
_____

R

Reflections or Observations:
_____
_____
_____

I

Inscribe the Selected Verse(s) in a different translation:
_____
_____
_____
_____
_____
_____

But He said, "On the contrary, blessed are those who hear the word of God and observe it." Luke 11:28

Lord, help me step out in obedience today…
_____
_____

"But a man must examine himself, and in so doing he is to eat of the bread and drink of the cup."
1 Corinthians 11:28

Lord, I would like to share and repent…
_____
_____

"For if you forgive others for their transgressions, your heavenly Father will also forgive you." Matthew 6:14

Lord, I need to forgive…
_____

**"O taste and see that the LORD is good;
How blessed is the man who takes refuge in Him!"** Psalm 34:8

Lord, I praise You for today's blessings...

"Ask, and it will be given to you; seek, and you will find; knock, and it will be opened to you." Matthew 7:7

Lord, hear my prayers …

Additional Scriptures:

Other Notes:

The Bible Reading Journal Series: 120 Days in the Bible.

**"Open my eyes, that I may behold
Wonderful things from Your law."**
Psalm 119:18

D

Date: _____

S

Selected Bible Passage: _____
_____
_____

R

Reflections or Observations: _____
_____
_____

I

Inscribe the Selected Verse(s) in a different translation:
_____
_____
_____
_____
_____
_____

But He said, "On the contrary, blessed are those who hear the word of God and observe it." Luke 11:28

Lord, help me step out in obedience today…
_____
_____

"But a man must examine himself, and in so doing he is to eat of the bread and drink of the cup."
1 Corinthians 11:28

Lord, I would like to share and repent…
_____
_____

"For if you forgive others for their transgressions, your heavenly Father will also forgive you." Matthew 6:14

Lord, I need to forgive…
_____

The Bible Reading Journal Series: 120 Days in the Bible.

"O taste and see that the LORD **is good;**
How blessed is the man who takes refuge in Him!" Psalm 34:8

Lord, I praise You for today's blessings...

"Ask, and it will be given to you; seek, and you will find; knock, and it will be opened to you." Matthew 7:7

Lord, hear my prayers …

Additional Scriptures:

Other Notes:

The Bible Reading Journal Series: 120 Days in the Bible.

**"Open my eyes, that I may behold
Wonderful things from Your law."**
Psalm 119:18

D

Date: _____

S

Selected Bible Passage:
_____
_____
_____

R

Reflections or Observations:
_____
_____
_____

I

Inscribe the Selected Verse(s) in a different translation:
_____
_____
_____
_____
_____
_____

But He said, "On the contrary, blessed are those who hear the word of God and observe it." Luke 11:28

Lord, help me step out in obedience today…
_____
_____

"But a man must examine himself, and in so doing he is to eat of the bread and drink of the cup."
1 Corinthians 11:28

Lord, I would like to share and repent…
_____
_____

"For if you forgive others for their transgressions, your heavenly Father will also forgive you." Matthew 6:14

Lord, I need to forgive…
_____

The Bible Reading Journal Series: 120 Days in the Bible.

**"O taste and see that the LORD is good;
How blessed is the man who takes refuge in Him!"** Psalm 34:8

Lord, I praise You for today's blessings...

"Ask, and it will be given to you; seek, and you will find; knock, and it will be opened to you." Matthew 7:7

Lord, hear my prayers …

Additional Scriptures:

Other Notes:

The Bible Reading Journal Series: 120 Days in the Bible.

**"Open my eyes, that I may behold
Wonderful things from Your law."**
Psalm 119:18

D

Date: _____

S

Selected Bible Passage:
_____
_____
_____

R

Reflections or Observations:
_____
_____
_____

I

Inscribe the Selected Verse(s) in a different translation:
_____
_____
_____
_____
_____
_____
_____

But He said, "On the contrary, blessed are those who hear the word of God and observe it." Luke 11:28

Lord, help me step out in obedience today…
_____
_____

"But a man must examine himself, and in so doing he is to eat of the bread and drink of the cup."
1 Corinthians 11:28

Lord, I would like to share and repent…
_____
_____

"For if you forgive others for their transgressions, your heavenly Father will also forgive you." Matthew 6:14

Lord, I need to forgive…
_____

The Bible Reading Journal Series: 120 Days in the Bible.

**"O taste and see that the Lord is good;
How blessed is the man who takes refuge in Him!"** Psalm 34:8

Lord, I praise You for today's blessings...

"Ask, and it will be given to you; seek, and you will find; knock, and it will be opened to you." Matthew 7:7

Lord, hear my prayers …

Additional Scriptures:

Other Notes:

The Bible Reading Journal Series: 120 Days in the Bible.

> **"Open my eyes, that I may behold
> Wonderful things from Your law."**
> Psalm 119:18

D

Date: _____

S

Selected Bible Passage:
_____
_____
_____

R

Reflections or Observations:
_____
_____
_____

I

Inscribe the Selected Verse(s) in a different translation:
_____
_____
_____
_____
_____
_____

But He said, "On the contrary, blessed are those who hear the word of God and observe it." Luke 11:28

Lord, help me step out in obedience today…
_____
_____

"But a man must examine himself, and in so doing he is to eat of the bread and drink of the cup."
1 Corinthians 11:28

Lord, I would like to share and repent…
_____
_____

"For if you forgive others for their transgressions, your heavenly Father will also forgive you." Matthew 6:14

Lord, I need to forgive…
_____

The Bible Reading Journal Series: 120 Days in the Bible.

**"O taste and see that the LORD is good;
How blessed is the man who takes refuge in Him!"** Psalm 34:8

Lord, I praise You for today's blessings...

"Ask, and it will be given to you; seek, and you will find; knock, and it will be opened to you." Matthew 7:7

Lord, hear my prayers …

Additional Scriptures:

Other Notes:

The Bible Reading Journal Series: 120 Days in the Bible.

**"Open my eyes, that I may behold
Wonderful things from Your law."**
Psalm 119:18

D

Date: _____

S

Selected Bible Passage:
_____
_____
_____

R

Reflections or Observations:
_____
_____
_____

I

Inscribe the Selected Verse(s) in a different translation:
_____
_____
_____
_____
_____
_____
_____

But He said, "On the contrary, blessed are those who hear the word of God and observe it." Luke 11:28

Lord, help me step out in obedience today…
_____
_____

"But a man must examine himself, and in so doing he is to eat of the bread and drink of the cup."
1 Corinthians 11:28

Lord, I would like to share and repent…
_____
_____

"For if you forgive others for their transgressions, your heavenly Father will also forgive you." Matthew 6:14

Lord, I need to forgive…
_____

The Bible Reading Journal Series: 120 Days in the Bible.

**"O taste and see that the LORD is good;
How blessed is the man who takes refuge in Him!"** Psalm 34:8

Lord, I praise You for today's blessings...

"Ask, and it will be given to you; seek, and you will find; knock, and it will be opened to you." Matthew 7:7

Lord, hear my prayers …

Additional Scriptures:

Other Notes:

The Bible Reading Journal Series: 120 Days in the Bible.

**"Open my eyes, that I may behold
Wonderful things from Your law."**
Psalm 119:18

D

Date: _____

S

Selected Bible Passage:
_____
_____
_____

R

Reflections or Observations:
_____
_____
_____

I

Inscribe the Selected Verse(s) in a different translation:
_____
_____
_____
_____
_____
_____
_____

But He said, "On the contrary, blessed are those who hear the word of God and observe it." Luke 11:28

Lord, help me step out in obedience today…
_____
_____

"But a man must examine himself, and in so doing he is to eat of the bread and drink of the cup."
1 Corinthians 11:28

Lord, I would like to share and repent…
_____
_____

"For if you forgive others for their transgressions, your heavenly Father will also forgive you." Matthew 6:14

Lord, I need to forgive…
_____

The Bible Reading Journal Series: 120 Days in the Bible.

**"O taste and see that the Lord is good;
How blessed is the man who takes refuge in Him!"** Psalm 34:8

Lord, I praise You for today's blessings...

"Ask, and it will be given to you; seek, and you will find; knock, and it will be opened to you." Matthew 7:7

Lord, hear my prayers …

Additional Scriptures:

Other Notes:

The Bible Reading Journal Series: 120 Days in the Bible.

> **"Open my eyes, that I may behold**
> **Wonderful things from Your law."**
> Psalm 119:18

D

Date: _____

S

Selected Bible Passage:
_____
_____
_____

R

Reflections or Observations:
_____
_____
_____

I

Inscribe the Selected Verse(s) in a different translation:
_____
_____
_____
_____
_____
_____

But He said, "On the contrary, blessed are those who hear the word of God and observe it." Luke 11:28

Lord, help me step out in obedience today…
_____
_____

"But a man must examine himself, and in so doing he is to eat of the bread and drink of the cup."
1 Corinthians 11:28

Lord, I would like to share and repent…
_____
_____

"For if you forgive others for their transgressions, your heavenly Father will also forgive you." Matthew 6:14

Lord, I need to forgive…
_____

The Bible Reading Journal Series: 120 Days in the Bible.

**"O taste and see that the Lord is good;
How blessed is the man who takes refuge in Him!"** Psalm 34:8

Lord, I praise You for today's blessings...

"Ask, and it will be given to you; seek, and you will find; knock, and it will be opened to you." Matthew 7:7

Lord, hear my prayers …

Additional Scriptures:

Other Notes:

The Bible Reading Journal Series: 120 Days in the Bible.

**"Open my eyes, that I may behold
Wonderful things from Your law."**
Psalm 119:18

D
Date: _____

S
Selected Bible Passage:
_____
_____
_____

R
Reflections or Observations:
_____
_____
_____

I
Inscribe the Selected Verse(s) in a different translation:
_____
_____
_____
_____
_____
_____
_____

But He said, "On the contrary, blessed are those who hear the word of God and observe it." Luke 11:28

Lord, help me step out in obedience today…
_____
_____

"But a man must examine himself, and in so doing he is to eat of the bread and drink of the cup."
1 Corinthians 11:28

Lord, I would like to share and repent…
_____
_____

"For if you forgive others for their transgressions, your heavenly Father will also forgive you." Matthew 6:14

Lord, I need to forgive…
_____

The Bible Reading Journal Series: 120 Days in the Bible.

**"O taste and see that the LORD is good;
How blessed is the man who takes refuge in Him!"** Psalm 34:8

Lord, I praise You for today's blessings...

"Ask, and it will be given to you; seek, and you will find; knock, and it will be opened to you." Matthew 7:7

Lord, hear my prayers …

Additional Scriptures:

Other Notes:

The Bible Reading Journal Series: 120 Days in the Bible.

**"Open my eyes, that I may behold
Wonderful things from Your law."**
Psalm 119:18

D

Date: _____

S

Selected Bible Passage:
_____
_____

R

Reflections or Observations:
_____
_____
_____

I

Inscribe the Selected Verse(s) in a different translation:
_____
_____
_____
_____
_____

But He said, "On the contrary, blessed are those who hear the word of God and observe it." Luke 11:28

Lord, help me step out in obedience today…
_____
_____

"But a man must examine himself, and in so doing he is to eat of the bread and drink of the cup."
1 Corinthians 11:28

Lord, I would like to share and repent…
_____
_____

"For if you forgive others for their transgressions, your heavenly Father will also forgive you." Matthew 6:14

Lord, I need to forgive…
_____

**"O taste and see that the Lord is good;
How blessed is the man who takes refuge in Him!"** Psalm 34:8

Lord, I praise You for today's blessings...

"Ask, and it will be given to you; seek, and you will find; knock, and it will be opened to you." Matthew 7:7

Lord, hear my prayers …

Additional Scriptures:

Other Notes:

The Bible Reading Journal Series: 120 Days in the Bible.

**"Open my eyes, that I may behold
Wonderful things from Your law."**
Psalm 119:18

D

Date: _____

S

Selected Bible Passage:
_____
_____
_____

R

Reflections or Observations:
_____
_____
_____

I

Inscribe the Selected Verse(s) in a different translation:
_____
_____
_____
_____
_____
_____

But He said, "On the contrary, blessed are those who hear the word of God and observe it." Luke 11:28

Lord, help me step out in obedience today…
_____
_____

"But a man must examine himself, and in so doing he is to eat of the bread and drink of the cup."
1 Corinthians 11:28

Lord, I would like to share and repent…
_____
_____

"For if you forgive others for their transgressions, your heavenly Father will also forgive you." Matthew 6:14

Lord, I need to forgive…
_____
_____

The Bible Reading Journal Series: 120 Days in the Bible.

**"O taste and see that the Lord is good;
How blessed is the man who takes refuge in Him!"** Psalm 34:8

Lord, I praise You for today's blessings...

"Ask, and it will be given to you; seek, and you will find; knock, and it will be opened to you." Matthew 7:7

Lord, hear my prayers …

Additional Scriptures:

Other Notes:

The Bible Reading Journal Series: 120 Days in the Bible.

**"Open my eyes, that I may behold
Wonderful things from Your law."**
Psalm 119:18

D

Date: _____

S

Selected Bible Passage:
_____
_____
_____

R

Reflections or Observations:
_____
_____
_____

I

Inscribe the Selected Verse(s) in a different translation:
_____
_____
_____
_____
_____
_____

But He said, "On the contrary, blessed are those who hear the word of God and observe it." Luke 11:28

Lord, help me step out in obedience today…
_____
_____

"But a man must examine himself, and in so doing he is to eat of the bread and drink of the cup."
1 Corinthians 11:28

Lord, I would like to share and repent…
_____
_____

"For if you forgive others for their transgressions, your heavenly Father will also forgive you." Matthew 6:14

Lord, I need to forgive…
_____

The Bible Reading Journal Series: 120 Days in the Bible.

"O taste and see that the LORD **is good;**
How blessed is the man who takes refuge in Him!" Psalm 34:8

Lord, I praise You for today's blessings...

"Ask, and it will be given to you; seek, and you will find; knock, and it will be opened to you." Matthew 7:7

Lord, hear my prayers …

Additional Scriptures:

Other Notes:

The Bible Reading Journal Series: 120 Days in the Bible.

**"Open my eyes, that I may behold
Wonderful things from Your law."**
Psalm 119:18

D

S Date: _____

Selected Bible Passage:
_____
_____
_____

R Reflections or Observations:
_____
_____
_____

I Inscribe the Selected Verse(s) in a different translation:
_____
_____
_____
_____
_____
_____
_____

But He said, "On the contrary, blessed are those who hear the word of God and observe it." Luke 11:28

Lord, help me step out in obedience today…
_____
_____

"But a man must examine himself, and in so doing he is to eat of the bread and drink of the cup."
1 Corinthians 11:28

Lord, I would like to share and repent…
_____
_____

"For if you forgive others for their transgressions, your heavenly Father will also forgive you." Matthew 6:14

Lord, I need to forgive…
_____

The Bible Reading Journal Series: 120 Days in the Bible.

"O taste and see that the LORD **is good;**
How blessed is the man who takes refuge in Him!" Psalm 34:8

Lord, I praise You for today's blessings...

"Ask, and it will be given to you; seek, and you will find; knock, and it will be opened to you." Matthew 7:7

Lord, hear my prayers …

Additional Scriptures:

Other Notes:

The Bible Reading Journal Series: 120 Days in the Bible.

**"Open my eyes, that I may behold
Wonderful things from Your law."**
Psalm 119:18

D

Date: _____

S

Selected Bible Passage: _____
_____
_____

R

Reflections or Observations: _____
_____
_____

I

Inscribe the Selected Verse(s) in a different translation:
_____
_____
_____
_____
_____
_____

But He said, "On the contrary, blessed are those who hear the word of God and observe it." Luke 11:28

Lord, help me step out in obedience today…
_____
_____

"But a man must examine himself, and in so doing he is to eat of the bread and drink of the cup."
1 Corinthians 11:28

Lord, I would like to share and repent…
_____
_____

"For if you forgive others for their transgressions, your heavenly Father will also forgive you." Matthew 6:14

Lord, I need to forgive…
_____

The Bible Reading Journal Series: 120 Days in the Bible.

"O taste and see that the LORD **is good;**
How blessed is the man who takes refuge in Him!" Psalm 34:8

Lord, I praise You for today's blessings...

"Ask, and it will be given to you; seek, and you will find; knock, and it will be opened to you." Matthew 7:7

Lord, hear my prayers …

Additional Scriptures:

Other Notes:

The Bible Reading Journal Series: 120 Days in the Bible.

**"Open my eyes, that I may behold
Wonderful things from Your law."**
Psalm 119:18

D

Date: _____

S

Selected Bible Passage:
_____
_____
_____

R

Reflections or Observations:
_____
_____
_____

I

Inscribe the Selected Verse(s) in a different translation:
_____
_____
_____
_____
_____
_____

But He said, "On the contrary, blessed are those who hear the word of God and observe it." Luke 11:28

Lord, help me step out in obedience today…
_____
_____

"But a man must examine himself, and in so doing he is to eat of the bread and drink of the cup."
1 Corinthians 11:28

Lord, I would like to share and repent…
_____
_____

"For if you forgive others for their transgressions, your heavenly Father will also forgive you." Matthew 6:14

Lord, I need to forgive…
_____

The Bible Reading Journal Series: 120 Days in the Bible.

**"O taste and see that the LORD is good;
How blessed is the man who takes refuge in Him!"** Psalm 34:8

Lord, I praise You for today's blessings...

"Ask, and it will be given to you; seek, and you will find; knock, and it will be opened to you." Matthew 7:7

Lord, hear my prayers …

Additional Scriptures:

Other Notes:

The Bible Reading Journal Series: 120 Days in the Bible.

**"Open my eyes, that I may behold
Wonderful things from Your law."**
Psalm 119:18

D

Date: _____

S

Selected Bible Passage:
_____
_____
_____

R

Reflections or Observations:
_____
_____
_____

I

Inscribe the Selected Verse(s) in a different translation:
_____
_____
_____
_____
_____
_____

But He said, "On the contrary, blessed are those who hear the word of God and observe it." Luke 11:28

Lord, help me step out in obedience today…
_____
_____

"But a man must examine himself, and in so doing he is to eat of the bread and drink of the cup."
1 Corinthians 11:28

Lord, I would like to share and repent…
_____
_____

"For if you forgive others for their transgressions, your heavenly Father will also forgive you." Matthew 6:14

Lord, I need to forgive…
_____

The Bible Reading Journal Series: 120 Days in the Bible.

**"O taste and see that the LORD is good;
How blessed is the man who takes refuge in Him!"** Psalm 34:8

Lord, I praise You for today's blessings...

"Ask, and it will be given to you; seek, and you will find; knock, and it will be opened to you." Matthew 7:7

Lord, hear my prayers …

Additional Scriptures:

Other Notes:

The Bible Reading Journal Series: 120 Days in the Bible.

> **"Open my eyes, that I may behold
> Wonderful things from Your law."**
> Psalm 119:18

D

Date: _____

S

Selected Bible Passage:
_____
_____
_____

R

Reflections or Observations:
_____
_____
_____

I

Inscribe the Selected Verse(s) in a different translation:
_____
_____
_____
_____
_____

But He said, "On the contrary, blessed are those who hear the word of God and observe it." Luke 11:28

Lord, help me step out in obedience today…
_____
_____

"But a man must examine himself, and in so doing he is to eat of the bread and drink of the cup."
1 Corinthians 11:28

Lord, I would like to share and repent…
_____
_____

"For if you forgive others for their transgressions, your heavenly Father will also forgive you." Matthew 6:14

Lord, I need to forgive…
_____

The Bible Reading Journal Series: 120 Days in the Bible.

**"O taste and see that the LORD is good;
How blessed is the man who takes refuge in Him!"** Psalm 34:8

Lord, I praise You for today's blessings...

"Ask, and it will be given to you; seek, and you will find; knock, and it will be opened to you." Matthew 7:7

Lord, hear my prayers …

Additional Scriptures:

Other Notes:

The Bible Reading Journal Series: 120 Days in the Bible.

**"Open my eyes, that I may behold
Wonderful things from Your law."**
Psalm 119:18

D

Date: _____

S

Selected Bible Passage:
_____
_____

R

Reflections or Observations:
_____
_____
_____

I

Inscribe the Selected Verse(s) in a different translation:
_____
_____
_____
_____
_____
_____

But He said, "On the contrary, blessed are those who hear the word of God and observe it." Luke 11:28

Lord, help me step out in obedience today…
_____
_____

"But a man must examine himself, and in so doing he is to eat of the bread and drink of the cup."
1 Corinthians 11:28

Lord, I would like to share and repent…
_____
_____

"For if you forgive others for their transgressions, your heavenly Father will also forgive you." Matthew 6:14

Lord, I need to forgive…
_____

The Bible Reading Journal Series: 120 Days in the Bible.

**"O taste and see that the LORD is good;
How blessed is the man who takes refuge in Him!"** Psalm 34:8

Lord, I praise You for today's blessings...

"Ask, and it will be given to you; seek, and you will find; knock, and it will be opened to you." Matthew 7:7

Lord, hear my prayers …

Additional Scriptures:

Other Notes:

The Bible Reading Journal Series: 120 Days in the Bible.

**"Open my eyes, that I may behold
Wonderful things from Your law."**
Psalm 119:18

D Date: _____

S Selected Bible Passage:
_____
_____
_____

R Reflections or Observations:
_____
_____
_____

I Inscribe the Selected Verse(s) in a different translation:
_____
_____
_____
_____
_____
_____

But He said, "On the contrary, blessed are those who hear the word of God and observe it." Luke 11:28

Lord, help me step out in obedience today…
_____
_____

"But a man must examine himself, and in so doing he is to eat of the bread and drink of the cup."
1 Corinthians 11:28

Lord, I would like to share and repent…
_____
_____

"For if you forgive others for their transgressions, your heavenly Father will also forgive you." Matthew 6:14

Lord, I need to forgive…
_____

**"O taste and see that the LORD is good;
How blessed is the man who takes refuge in Him!"** Psalm 34:8

Lord, I praise You for today's blessings...

"Ask, and it will be given to you; seek, and you will find; knock, and it will be opened to you." Matthew 7:7

Lord, hear my prayers …

Additional Scriptures:

Other Notes:

The Bible Reading Journal Series: 120 Days in the Bible.

**"Open my eyes, that I may behold
Wonderful things from Your law."**
Psalm 119:18

D

Date: _____

S

Selected Bible Passage:
_____
_____
_____

R

Reflections or Observations:
_____
_____
_____

I

Inscribe the Selected Verse(s) in a different translation:
_____
_____
_____
_____
_____
_____
_____

But He said, "On the contrary, blessed are those who hear the word of God and observe it." Luke 11:28

Lord, help me step out in obedience today…
_____
_____

"But a man must examine himself, and in so doing he is to eat of the bread and drink of the cup."
1 Corinthians 11:28

Lord, I would like to share and repent…
_____
_____

"For if you forgive others for their transgressions, your heavenly Father will also forgive you." Matthew 6:14

Lord, I need to forgive…
_____

The Bible Reading Journal Series: 120 Days in the Bible.

"O taste and see that the LORD **is good;
How blessed is the man who takes refuge in Him!"** Psalm 34:8

Lord, I praise You for today's blessings...

"Ask, and it will be given to you; seek, and you will find; knock, and it will be opened to you." Matthew 7:7

Lord, hear my prayers …

Additional Scriptures:

Other Notes:

The Bible Reading Journal Series: 120 Days in the Bible.

**"Open my eyes, that I may behold
Wonderful things from Your law."**
Psalm 119:18

D

Date: _____

S

Selected Bible Passage:
_____
_____
_____

R

Reflections or Observations:
_____
_____
_____

I

Inscribe the Selected Verse(s) in a different translation:
_____
_____
_____
_____
_____
_____
_____

But He said, "On the contrary, blessed are those who hear the word of God and observe it." Luke 11:28

Lord, help me step out in obedience today…
_____
_____

"But a man must examine himself, and in so doing he is to eat of the bread and drink of the cup."
1 Corinthians 11:28

Lord, I would like to share and repent…
_____
_____

"For if you forgive others for their transgressions, your heavenly Father will also forgive you." Matthew 6:14

Lord, I need to forgive…
_____

The Bible Reading Journal Series: 120 Days in the Bible.

**"O taste and see that the LORD is good;
How blessed is the man who takes refuge in Him!"** Psalm 34:8

Lord, I praise You for today's blessings...

"Ask, and it will be given to you; seek, and you will find; knock, and it will be opened to you." Matthew 7:7

Lord, hear my prayers ...

Additional Scriptures:

Other Notes:

The Bible Reading Journal Series: 120 Days in the Bible.

**"Open my eyes, that I may behold
Wonderful things from Your law."**
Psalm 119:18

D

Date: _____

S

Selected Bible Passage:
_____
_____
_____

R

Reflections or Observations:
_____
_____
_____

I

Inscribe the Selected Verse(s) in a different translation:
_____
_____
_____
_____
_____
_____
_____

But He said, "On the contrary, blessed are those who hear the word of God and observe it." Luke 11:28

Lord, help me step out in obedience today…
_____
_____

"But a man must examine himself, and in so doing he is to eat of the bread and drink of the cup."
1 Corinthians 11:28

Lord, I would like to share and repent…
_____
_____

"For if you forgive others for their transgressions, your heavenly Father will also forgive you." Matthew 6:14

Lord, I need to forgive…
_____

The Bible Reading Journal Series: 120 Days in the Bible.

**"O taste and see that the LORD is good;
How blessed is the man who takes refuge in Him!"** Psalm 34:8

Lord, I praise You for today's blessings...

"Ask, and it will be given to you; seek, and you will find; knock, and it will be opened to you." Matthew 7:7

Lord, hear my prayers …

Additional Scriptures:

Other Notes:

The Bible Reading Journal Series: 120 Days in the Bible.

**"Open my eyes, that I may behold
Wonderful things from Your law."**
Psalm 119:18

D

Date: _____

S

Selected Bible Passage:
_____
_____
_____

R

Reflections or Observations:
_____
_____
_____

I

Inscribe the Selected Verse(s) in a different translation:
_____
_____
_____
_____
_____
_____
_____

But He said, "On the contrary, blessed are those who hear the word of God and observe it." Luke 11:28

Lord, help me step out in obedience today…
_____
_____

"But a man must examine himself, and in so doing he is to eat of the bread and drink of the cup."
1 Corinthians 11:28

Lord, I would like to share and repent…
_____
_____

"For if you forgive others for their transgressions, your heavenly Father will also forgive you." Matthew 6:14

Lord, I need to forgive…
_____

The Bible Reading Journal Series: 120 Days in the Bible.

> **"O taste and see that the LORD is good;**
> **How blessed is the man who takes refuge in Him!"** Psalm 34:8

Lord, I praise You for today's blessings...

"Ask, and it will be given to you; seek, and you will find; knock, and it will be opened to you." Matthew 7:7

Lord, hear my prayers …

Additional Scriptures:

Other Notes:

The Bible Reading Journal Series: 120 Days in the Bible.

**"Open my eyes, that I may behold
Wonderful things from Your law."**
Psalm 119:18

D

Date: _____

S

Selected Bible Passage:
_____
_____
_____

R

Reflections or Observations:
_____
_____
_____

I

Inscribe the Selected Verse(s) in a different translation:
_____
_____
_____
_____
_____
_____
_____

But He said, "On the contrary, blessed are those who hear the word of God and observe it." Luke 11:28

Lord, help me step out in obedience today…
_____
_____

"But a man must examine himself, and in so doing he is to eat of the bread and drink of the cup."
1 Corinthians 11:28

Lord, I would like to share and repent…
_____
_____

"For if you forgive others for their transgressions, your heavenly Father will also forgive you." Matthew 6:14

Lord, I need to forgive…
_____

The Bible Reading Journal Series: 120 Days in the Bible.

"O taste and see that the LORD **is good;**
How blessed is the man who takes refuge in Him!" Psalm 34:8

Lord, I praise You for today's blessings...

"Ask, and it will be given to you; seek, and you will find; knock, and it will be opened to you." Matthew 7:7

Lord, hear my prayers ...

Additional Scriptures:

Other Notes:

The Bible Reading Journal Series: 120 Days in the Bible.

> **"Open my eyes, that I may behold
> Wonderful things from Your law."**
> Psalm 119:18

D

Date: _____

S

Selected Bible Passage:
_____
_____
_____

R

Reflections or Observations:
_____
_____
_____

I

Inscribe the Selected Verse(s) in a different translation:
_____
_____
_____
_____
_____
_____

But He said, "On the contrary, blessed are those who hear the word of God and observe it." Luke 11:28

Lord, help me step out in obedience today…
_____
_____

"But a man must examine himself, and in so doing he is to eat of the bread and drink of the cup."
1 Corinthians 11:28

Lord, I would like to share and repent…
_____
_____

"For if you forgive others for their transgressions, your heavenly Father will also forgive you." Matthew 6:14

Lord, I need to forgive…
_____

The Bible Reading Journal Series: 120 Days in the Bible.

**"O taste and see that the LORD is good;
How blessed is the man who takes refuge in Him!"** Psalm 34:8

Lord, I praise You for today's blessings...

"Ask, and it will be given to you; seek, and you will find; knock, and it will be opened to you." Matthew 7:7

Lord, hear my prayers …

Additional Scriptures:

Other Notes:

The Bible Reading Journal Series: 120 Days in the Bible.

> **"Open my eyes, that I may behold**
> **Wonderful things from Your law."**
> Psalm 119:18

D

Date: _____

S

Selected Bible Passage:
_____
_____
_____

R

Reflections or Observations:
_____
_____
_____

I

Inscribe the Selected Verse(s) in a different translation:
_____
_____
_____
_____
_____
_____
_____

But He said, "On the contrary, blessed are those who hear the word of God and observe it." Luke 11:28

Lord, help me step out in obedience today…
_____
_____

"But a man must examine himself, and in so doing he is to eat of the bread and drink of the cup."
1 Corinthians 11:28

Lord, I would like to share and repent…
_____
_____

"For if you forgive others for their transgressions, your heavenly Father will also forgive you." Matthew 6:14

Lord, I need to forgive…
_____

The Bible Reading Journal Series: 120 Days in the Bible.

**"O taste and see that the LORD is good;
How blessed is the man who takes refuge in Him!"** Psalm 34:8

Lord, I praise You for today's blessings...

"Ask, and it will be given to you; seek, and you will find; knock, and it will be opened to you." Matthew 7:7

Lord, hear my prayers …

Additional Scriptures:

Other Notes:

The Bible Reading Journal Series: 120 Days in the Bible.

**"Open my eyes, that I may behold
Wonderful things from Your law."**
Psalm 119:18

D

Date: _____

S

Selected Bible Passage:
_____
_____
_____

R

Reflections or Observations:
_____
_____
_____

I

Inscribe the Selected Verse(s) in a different translation:
_____
_____
_____
_____
_____
_____
_____

But He said, "On the contrary, blessed are those who hear the word of God and observe it." Luke 11:28

Lord, help me step out in obedience today…
_____
_____

"But a man must examine himself, and in so doing he is to eat of the bread and drink of the cup."
1 Corinthians 11:28

Lord, I would like to share and repent…
_____
_____

"For if you forgive others for their transgressions, your heavenly Father will also forgive you." Matthew 6:14

Lord, I need to forgive…
_____

The Bible Reading Journal Series: 120 Days in the Bible.

**"O taste and see that the LORD is good;
How blessed is the man who takes refuge in Him!"** Psalm 34:8

Lord, I praise You for today's blessings...

"Ask, and it will be given to you; seek, and you will find; knock, and it will be opened to you." Matthew 7:7

Lord, hear my prayers …

Additional Scriptures:

Other Notes:

The Bible Reading Journal Series: 120 Days in the Bible.

**"Open my eyes, that I may behold
Wonderful things from Your law."**
Psalm 119:18

D

Date: _____

S

Selected Bible Passage:
_____
_____
_____

R

Reflections or Observations:
_____
_____
_____

I

Inscribe the Selected Verse(s) in a different translation:
_____
_____
_____
_____
_____
_____
_____

But He said, "On the contrary, blessed are those who hear the word of God and observe it." Luke 11:28

Lord, help me step out in obedience today…
_____
_____

"But a man must examine himself, and in so doing he is to eat of the bread and drink of the cup."
1 Corinthians 11:28

Lord, I would like to share and repent…
_____
_____

"For if you forgive others for their transgressions, your heavenly Father will also forgive you." Matthew 6:14

Lord, I need to forgive…
_____

The Bible Reading Journal Series: 120 Days in the Bible.

"O taste and see that the LORD **is good;**
How blessed is the man who takes refuge in Him!" Psalm 34:8

Lord, I praise You for today's blessings...

"Ask, and it will be given to you; seek, and you will find; knock, and it will be opened to you." Matthew 7:7

Lord, hear my prayers …

Additional Scriptures:

Other Notes:

The Bible Reading Journal Series: 120 Days in the Bible.

**"Open my eyes, that I may behold
Wonderful things from Your law."**
Psalm 119:18

D

Date: _____

S

Selected Bible Passage:
_____
_____
_____

R

Reflections or Observations:
_____
_____
_____

I

Inscribe the Selected Verse(s) in a different translation:
_____
_____
_____
_____
_____
_____
_____

But He said, "On the contrary, blessed are those who hear the word of God and observe it." Luke 11:28

Lord, help me step out in obedience today…
_____
_____

"But a man must examine himself, and in so doing he is to eat of the bread and drink of the cup."
1 Corinthians 11:28

Lord, I would like to share and repent…
_____
_____

"For if you forgive others for their transgressions, your heavenly Father will also forgive you." Matthew 6:14

Lord, I need to forgive…
_____

The Bible Reading Journal Series: 120 Days in the Bible.

**"O taste and see that the LORD is good;
How blessed is the man who takes refuge in Him!"** Psalm 34:8

Lord, I praise You for today's blessings...

"Ask, and it will be given to you; seek, and you will find; knock, and it will be opened to you." Matthew 7:7

Lord, hear my prayers ...

Additional Scriptures:

Other Notes:

The Bible Reading Journal Series: 120 Days in the Bible.

> **"Open my eyes, that I may behold
> Wonderful things from Your law."**
> Psalm 119:18

D

Date: _____

S

Selected Bible Passage:
_____
_____
_____

R

Reflections or Observations:
_____
_____
_____

I

Inscribe the Selected Verse(s) in a different translation:
_____
_____
_____
_____
_____
_____

But He said, "On the contrary, blessed are those who hear the word of God and observe it." Luke 11:28

Lord, help me step out in obedience today…
_____
_____

"But a man must examine himself, and in so doing he is to eat of the bread and drink of the cup."
1 Corinthians 11:28

Lord, I would like to share and repent…
_____
_____

"For if you forgive others for their transgressions, your heavenly Father will also forgive you." Matthew 6:14

Lord, I need to forgive…
_____

**"O taste and see that the LORD is good;
How blessed is the man who takes refuge in Him!"** Psalm 34:8

Lord, I praise You for today's blessings...

"**Ask, and it will be given to you; seek, and you will find; knock, and it will be opened to you.**" Matthew 7:7

Lord, hear my prayers ...

Additional Scriptures:

Other Notes:

The Bible Reading Journal Series: 120 Days in the Bible.

**"Open my eyes, that I may behold
Wonderful things from Your law."**
Psalm 119:18

D Date: _____

S Selected Bible Passage:
_____
_____

R Reflections or Observations:
_____
_____

I Inscribe the Selected Verse(s) in a different translation:
_____
_____
_____
_____
_____
_____

But He said, "On the contrary, blessed are those who hear the word of God and observe it." Luke 11:28

Lord, help me step out in obedience today…
_____
_____

"But a man must examine himself, and in so doing he is to eat of the bread and drink of the cup."
1 Corinthians 11:28

Lord, I would like to share and repent…
_____
_____

"For if you forgive others for their transgressions, your heavenly Father will also forgive you." Matthew 6:14

Lord, I need to forgive…
_____

The Bible Reading Journal Series: 120 Days in the Bible.

**"O taste and see that the LORD is good;
How blessed is the man who takes refuge in Him!"** Psalm 34:8

Lord, I praise You for today's blessings...

"Ask, and it will be given to you; seek, and you will find; knock, and it will be opened to you." Matthew 7:7

Lord, hear my prayers …

Additional Scriptures:

Other Notes:

The Bible Reading Journal Series: 120 Days in the Bible.

> **"Open my eyes, that I may behold
> Wonderful things from Your law."**
> Psalm 119:18

D Date: _____

S Selected Bible Passage:
_____
_____
_____

R Reflections or Observations:
_____
_____
_____

I Inscribe the Selected Verse(s) in a different translation:
_____
_____
_____
_____
_____
_____
_____

But He said, "On the contrary, blessed are those who hear the word of God and observe it." Luke 11:28

Lord, help me step out in obedience today…
_____
_____

"But a man must examine himself, and in so doing he is to eat of the bread and drink of the cup."
1 Corinthians 11:28

Lord, I would like to share and repent…
_____
_____

"For if you forgive others for their transgressions, your heavenly Father will also forgive you." Matthew 6:14

Lord, I need to forgive…
_____

The Bible Reading Journal Series: 120 Days in the Bible.

**"O taste and see that the LORD is good;
How blessed is the man who takes refuge in Him!"** Psalm 34:8

Lord, I praise You for today's blessings...

"Ask, and it will be given to you; seek, and you will find; knock, and it will be opened to you." Matthew 7:7

Lord, hear my prayers …

Additional Scriptures:

Other Notes:

The Bible Reading Journal Series: 120 Days in the Bible.

**"Open my eyes, that I may behold
Wonderful things from Your law."**
Psalm 119:18

D

Date: _____

S

Selected Bible Passage:
_____
_____
_____

R

Reflections or Observations:
_____
_____
_____

I

Inscribe the Selected Verse(s) in a different translation:
_____
_____
_____
_____
_____
_____
_____

But He said, "On the contrary, blessed are those who hear the word of God and observe it." Luke 11:28

Lord, help me step out in obedience today…
_____
_____

"But a man must examine himself, and in so doing he is to eat of the bread and drink of the cup."
1 Corinthians 11:28

Lord, I would like to share and repent…
_____
_____

"For if you forgive others for their transgressions, your heavenly Father will also forgive you." Matthew 6:14

Lord, I need to forgive…
_____

**"O taste and see that the LORD is good;
How blessed is the man who takes refuge in Him!"** Psalm 34:8

Lord, I praise You for today's blessings...

"Ask, and it will be given to you; seek, and you will find; knock, and it will be opened to you." Matthew 7:7

Lord, hear my prayers …

Additional Scriptures:

Other Notes:

The Bible Reading Journal Series: 120 Days in the Bible.

**"Open my eyes, that I may behold
Wonderful things from Your law."**
Psalm 119:18

D

Date: _____

S

Selected Bible Passage: _____
_____
_____

R

Reflections or Observations: _____
_____
_____

I

Inscribe the Selected Verse(s) in a different translation:
_____
_____
_____
_____
_____
_____

But He said, "On the contrary, blessed are those who hear the word of God and observe it." Luke 11:28

Lord, help me step out in obedience today…
_____
_____

"But a man must examine himself, and in so doing he is to eat of the bread and drink of the cup."
1 Corinthians 11:28

Lord, I would like to share and repent…
_____
_____

"For if you forgive others for their transgressions, your heavenly Father will also forgive you." Matthew 6:14

Lord, I need to forgive…
_____
_____

The Bible Reading Journal Series: 120 Days in the Bible.

**"O taste and see that the LORD is good;
How blessed is the man who takes refuge in Him!"** Psalm 34:8

Lord, I praise You for today's blessings...

"Ask, and it will be given to you; seek, and you will find; knock, and it will be opened to you." Matthew 7:7

Lord, hear my prayers …

Additional Scriptures:

Other Notes:

The Bible Reading Journal Series: 120 Days in the Bible.

**"Open my eyes, that I may behold
Wonderful things from Your law."**
Psalm 119:18

D

Date: _____

S

Selected Bible Passage:
_____
_____
_____

R

Reflections or Observations:
_____
_____
_____
_____

I

Inscribe the Selected Verse(s) in a different translation:
_____
_____
_____
_____
_____
_____

But He said, "On the contrary, blessed are those who hear the word of God and observe it." Luke 11:28

Lord, help me step out in obedience today…
_____
_____

"But a man must examine himself, and in so doing he is to eat of the bread and drink of the cup."
1 Corinthians 11:28

Lord, I would like to share and repent…
_____
_____

"For if you forgive others for their transgressions, your heavenly Father will also forgive you." Matthew 6:14

Lord, I need to forgive…
_____

**"O taste and see that the LORD is good;
How blessed is the man who takes refuge in Him!"** Psalm 34:8

Lord, I praise You for today's blessings...

"Ask, and it will be given to you; seek, and you will find; knock, and it will be opened to you." Matthew 7:7

Lord, hear my prayers …

Additional Scriptures:

Other Notes:

The Bible Reading Journal Series: 120 Days in the Bible.

**"Open my eyes, that I may behold
Wonderful things from Your law."**
Psalm 119:18

D

Date: _____

S

Selected Bible Passage:
_____
_____
_____

R

Reflections or Observations:
_____
_____
_____

I

Inscribe the Selected Verse(s) in a different translation:
_____
_____
_____
_____
_____
_____
_____

But He said, "On the contrary, blessed are those who hear the word of God and observe it." Luke 11:28

Lord, help me step out in obedience today…
_____
_____

"But a man must examine himself, and in so doing he is to eat of the bread and drink of the cup."
1 Corinthians 11:28

Lord, I would like to share and repent…
_____
_____

"For if you forgive others for their transgressions, your heavenly Father will also forgive you." Matthew 6:14

Lord, I need to forgive…
_____

The Bible Reading Journal Series: 120 Days in the Bible.

"O taste and see that the LORD **is good;**
How blessed is the man who takes refuge in Him!" Psalm 34:8

Lord, I praise You for today's blessings...

_____
_____

"Ask, and it will be given to you; seek, and you will find; knock, and it will be opened to you." Matthew 7:7

Lord, hear my prayers …

_____
_____
_____
_____

Additional Scriptures:

_____
_____
_____
_____
_____
_____
_____
_____
_____

Other Notes:

_____
_____
_____
_____
_____
_____
_____
_____
_____
_____
_____
_____
_____
_____
_____
_____

The Bible Reading Journal Series: 120 Days in the Bible.

**"Open my eyes, that I may behold
Wonderful things from Your law."**
Psalm 119:18

D

Date: _____

S

Selected Bible Passage:
_____
_____
_____

R

Reflections or Observations:
_____
_____
_____

I

Inscribe the Selected Verse(s) in a different translation:
_____
_____
_____
_____
_____
_____
_____

But He said, "On the contrary, blessed are those who hear the word of God and observe it." Luke 11:28

Lord, help me step out in obedience today…
_____
_____

"But a man must examine himself, and in so doing he is to eat of the bread and drink of the cup."
1 Corinthians 11:28

Lord, I would like to share and repent…
_____
_____

"For if you forgive others for their transgressions, your heavenly Father will also forgive you." Matthew 6:14

Lord, I need to forgive…
_____

The Bible Reading Journal Series: 120 Days in the Bible.

**"O taste and see that the LORD is good;
How blessed is the man who takes refuge in Him!"** Psalm 34:8

Lord, I praise You for today's blessings...

"Ask, and it will be given to you; seek, and you will find; knock, and it will be opened to you." Matthew 7:7

Lord, hear my prayers …

Additional Scriptures:

Other Notes:

The Bible Reading Journal Series: 120 Days in the Bible.

**"Open my eyes, that I may behold
Wonderful things from Your law."**
Psalm 119:18

D

Date: _____

S

Selected Bible Passage:
_____
_____
_____

R

Reflections or Observations:
_____
_____
_____

I

Inscribe the Selected Verse(s) in a different translation:
_____
_____
_____
_____
_____
_____
_____

But He said, "On the contrary, blessed are those who hear the word of God and observe it." Luke 11:28

Lord, help me step out in obedience today…
_____
_____

"But a man must examine himself, and in so doing he is to eat of the bread and drink of the cup."
1 Corinthians 11:28

Lord, I would like to share and repent…
_____
_____

"For if you forgive others for their transgressions, your heavenly Father will also forgive you." Matthew 6:14

Lord, I need to forgive…
_____

The Bible Reading Journal Series: 120 Days in the Bible.

**"O taste and see that the LORD is good;
How blessed is the man who takes refuge in Him!"** Psalm 34:8

Lord, I praise You for today's blessings...

"Ask, and it will be given to you; seek, and you will find; knock, and it will be opened to you." Matthew 7:7

Lord, hear my prayers …

Additional Scriptures:

Other Notes:

The Bible Reading Journal Series: 120 Days in the Bible.

> **"Open my eyes, that I may behold
> Wonderful things from Your law."**
> Psalm 119:18

D

Date: _____

S

Selected Bible Passage:
_____
_____
_____

R

Reflections or Observations:
_____
_____
_____

I

Inscribe the Selected Verse(s) in a different translation:
_____
_____
_____
_____
_____
_____
_____

But He said, "On the contrary, blessed are those who hear the word of God and observe it." Luke 11:28

Lord, help me step out in obedience today…
_____
_____

"But a man must examine himself, and in so doing he is to eat of the bread and drink of the cup."
1 Corinthians 11:28

Lord, I would like to share and repent…
_____
_____

"For if you forgive others for their transgressions, your heavenly Father will also forgive you." Matthew 6:14

Lord, I need to forgive…
_____

The Bible Reading Journal Series: 120 Days in the Bible.

**"O taste and see that the LORD is good;
How blessed is the man who takes refuge in Him!"** Psalm 34:8

Lord, I praise You for today's blessings...

"Ask, and it will be given to you; seek, and you will find; knock, and it will be opened to you." Matthew 7:7

Lord, hear my prayers …

Additional Scriptures:

Other Notes:

The Bible Reading Journal Series: 120 Days in the Bible.

**"Open my eyes, that I may behold
Wonderful things from Your law."**
Psalm 119:18

D

Date: _____

S

Selected Bible Passage:
_____
_____
_____

R

Reflections or Observations:
_____
_____
_____

I

Inscribe the Selected Verse(s) in a different translation:
_____
_____
_____
_____
_____
_____

But He said, "On the contrary, blessed are those who hear the word of God and observe it." Luke 11:28

Lord, help me step out in obedience today…
_____
_____

"But a man must examine himself, and in so doing he is to eat of the bread and drink of the cup."
1 Corinthians 11:28

Lord, I would like to share and repent…
_____
_____

"For if you forgive others for their transgressions, your heavenly Father will also forgive you." Matthew 6:14

Lord, I need to forgive…
_____

The Bible Reading Journal Series: 120 Days in the Bible.

"O taste and see that the LORD **is good;
How blessed is the man who takes refuge in Him!"** Psalm 34:8

Lord, I praise You for today's blessings...

"Ask, and it will be given to you; seek, and you will find; knock, and it will be opened to you." Matthew 7:7

Lord, hear my prayers …

Additional Scriptures:

Other Notes:

The Bible Reading Journal Series: 120 Days in the Bible.

**"Open my eyes, that I may behold
Wonderful things from Your law."**
Psalm 119:18

D
Date: _____

S
Selected Bible Passage:
_____
_____
_____

R
Reflections or Observations:
_____
_____
_____

I
Inscribe the Selected Verse(s) in a different translation:
_____
_____
_____
_____
_____
_____
_____

But He said, "On the contrary, blessed are those who hear the word of God and observe it." Luke 11:28

Lord, help me step out in obedience today…
_____
_____

"But a man must examine himself, and in so doing he is to eat of the bread and drink of the cup."
1 Corinthians 11:28

Lord, I would like to share and repent…
_____
_____

"For if you forgive others for their transgressions, your heavenly Father will also forgive you." Matthew 6:14

Lord, I need to forgive…
_____

**"O taste and see that the LORD is good;
How blessed is the man who takes refuge in Him!"** Psalm 34:8

Lord, I praise You for today's blessings...

"Ask, and it will be given to you; seek, and you will find; knock, and it will be opened to you." Matthew 7:7

Lord, hear my prayers …

Additional Scriptures:

Other Notes:

The Bible Reading Journal Series: 120 Days in the Bible.

**"Open my eyes, that I may behold
Wonderful things from Your law."**
Psalm 119:18

D

Date: _____

S

Selected Bible Passage:
_____
_____
_____

R

Reflections or Observations:
_____
_____
_____

I

Inscribe the Selected Verse(s) in a different translation:
_____
_____
_____
_____
_____
_____
_____

But He said, "On the contrary, blessed are those who hear the word of God and observe it." Luke 11:28

Lord, help me step out in obedience today…
_____
_____

"But a man must examine himself, and in so doing he is to eat of the bread and drink of the cup."
1 Corinthians 11:28

Lord, I would like to share and repent…
_____
_____

"For if you forgive others for their transgressions, your heavenly Father will also forgive you." Matthew 6:14

Lord, I need to forgive…
_____

The Bible Reading Journal Series: 120 Days in the Bible.

"O taste and see that the LORD is good;
How blessed is the man who takes refuge in Him!" Psalm 34:8

Lord, I praise You for today's blessings...

___

"Ask, and it will be given to you; seek, and you will find; knock, and it will be opened to you." Matthew 7:7

Lord, hear my prayers …

___

Additional Scriptures:

___

Other Notes:

___

The Bible Reading Journal Series: 120 Days in the Bible.

**"Open my eyes, that I may behold
Wonderful things from Your law."**
Psalm 119:18

D

Date: _____

S

Selected Bible Passage:
_____
_____
_____

R

Reflections or Observations:
_____
_____
_____

I

Inscribe the Selected Verse(s) in a different translation:
_____
_____
_____
_____
_____
_____
_____

But He said, "On the contrary, blessed are those who hear the word of God and observe it." Luke 11:28

Lord, help me step out in obedience today…
_____
_____

"But a man must examine himself, and in so doing he is to eat of the bread and drink of the cup."
1 Corinthians 11:28

Lord, I would like to share and repent…
_____
_____

"For if you forgive others for their transgressions, your heavenly Father will also forgive you." Matthew 6:14

Lord, I need to forgive…
_____

**"O taste and see that the LORD is good;
How blessed is the man who takes refuge in Him!"** Psalm 34:8

Lord, I praise You for today's blessings...

"Ask, and it will be given to you; seek, and you will find; knock, and it will be opened to you." Matthew 7:7

Lord, hear my prayers …

Additional Scriptures:

Other Notes:

The Bible Reading Journal Series: 120 Days in the Bible.

**"Open my eyes, that I may behold
Wonderful things from Your law."**
Psalm 119:18

D Date: _____

S Selected Bible Passage:
_____
_____
_____

R Reflections or Observations:
_____
_____
_____

I Inscribe the Selected Verse(s) in a different translation:
_____
_____
_____
_____
_____
_____

But He said, "On the contrary, blessed are those who hear the word of God and observe it." Luke 11:28

Lord, help me step out in obedience today…
_____
_____

"But a man must examine himself, and in so doing he is to eat of the bread and drink of the cup."
1 Corinthians 11:28

Lord, I would like to share and repent…
_____
_____

"For if you forgive others for their transgressions, your heavenly Father will also forgive you." Matthew 6:14

Lord, I need to forgive…
_____

The Bible Reading Journal Series: 120 Days in the Bible.

"O taste and see that the LORD** is good;
How blessed is the man who takes refuge in Him!"** Psalm 34:8

Lord, I praise You for today's blessings...

"**Ask, and it will be given to you; seek, and you will find; knock, and it will be opened to you.**" Matthew 7:7

Lord, hear my prayers …

Additional Scriptures:

Other Notes:

The Bible Reading Journal Series: 120 Days in the Bible.

**"Open my eyes, that I may behold
Wonderful things from Your law."**
Psalm 119:18

D

Date: _____

S

Selected Bible Passage:
_____
_____
_____

R

Reflections or Observations:
_____
_____
_____

I

Inscribe the Selected Verse(s) in a different translation:
_____
_____
_____
_____
_____
_____
_____

But He said, "On the contrary, blessed are those who hear the word of God and observe it." Luke 11:28

Lord, help me step out in obedience today…
_____
_____

"But a man must examine himself, and in so doing he is to eat of the bread and drink of the cup."
1 Corinthians 11:28

Lord, I would like to share and repent…
_____
_____

"For if you forgive others for their transgressions, your heavenly Father will also forgive you." Matthew 6:14

Lord, I need to forgive…
_____

The Bible Reading Journal Series: 120 Days in the Bible.

"O taste and see that the LORD **is good;**
How blessed is the man who takes refuge in Him!" Psalm 34:8

Lord, I praise You for today's blessings...

"Ask, and it will be given to you; seek, and you will find; knock, and it will be opened to you." Matthew 7:7

Lord, hear my prayers …

Additional Scriptures:

Other Notes:

The Bible Reading Journal Series: 120 Days in the Bible.

**"Open my eyes, that I may behold
Wonderful things from Your law."**
Psalm 119:18

D Date: _____

S Selected Bible Passage:
_____
_____
_____

R Reflections or Observations:
_____
_____
_____

I Inscribe the Selected Verse(s) in a different translation:
_____
_____
_____
_____
_____
_____
_____

But He said, "On the contrary, blessed are those who hear the word of God and observe it." Luke 11:28

Lord, help me step out in obedience today…
_____
_____

"But a man must examine himself, and in so doing he is to eat of the bread and drink of the cup."
1 Corinthians 11:28

Lord, I would like to share and repent…
_____
_____

"For if you forgive others for their transgressions, your heavenly Father will also forgive you." Matthew 6:14

Lord, I need to forgive…
_____

The Bible Reading Journal Series: 120 Days in the Bible.

"O taste and see that the LORD **is good;**
How blessed is the man who takes refuge in Him!" Psalm 34:8

Lord, I praise You for today's blessings...

"Ask, and it will be given to you; seek, and you will find; knock, and it will be opened to you." Matthew 7:7

Lord, hear my prayers …

Additional Scriptures:

Other Notes:

The Bible Reading Journal Series: 120 Days in the Bible.

**"Open my eyes, that I may behold
Wonderful things from Your law."**
Psalm 119:18

D

Date: _____

S

Selected Bible Passage:
_____
_____
_____

R

Reflections or Observations:
_____
_____
_____

I

Inscribe the Selected Verse(s) in a different translation:
_____
_____
_____
_____
_____
_____
_____

But He said, "On the contrary, blessed are those who hear the word of God and observe it." Luke 11:28

Lord, help me step out in obedience today…
_____
_____

"But a man must examine himself, and in so doing he is to eat of the bread and drink of the cup."
1 Corinthians 11:28

Lord, I would like to share and repent…
_____
_____

"For if you forgive others for their transgressions, your heavenly Father will also forgive you." Matthew 6:14

Lord, I need to forgive…
_____

The Bible Reading Journal Series: 120 Days in the Bible.

"O taste and see that the LORD is good;
How blessed is the man who takes refuge in Him!" Psalm 34:8

Lord, I praise You for today's blessings...

"Ask, and it will be given to you; seek, and you will find; knock, and it will be opened to you." Matthew 7:7

Lord, hear my prayers …

Additional Scriptures:

Other Notes:

The Bible Reading Journal Series: 120 Days in the Bible.

ABOUT THE AUTHOR

Adriana Morales-Spokane was born in Venezuela. She relocated to the United States at a young age and lived in Florida for twenty-six years. She visits her family and friends in Miami yearly and delights herself with Cuban meals.

Adriana now lives with her husband in Collierville, Tennessee and works full-time in a leadership role with the State.

Adriana enjoys adult coloring, creative Bible journaling, piano playing and blogging for KeynotesinHisPresence.org

What is her favorite time of day? Adriana enjoys waking up at sunrise to read her Bible, her devotionals, and prayers.

For over a decade, Adriana delights in serving faithfully in discipleship communities. Her motto is "Truth in action." She is passionate about The Great Commission.

Professionally, Adriana has been in the mental health field for over twenty-six years and has faithfully served children, adolescents and their families as well as adults with intellectual disabilities (ID) and Autism Spectrum Disorder (ASD). She worked as a Licensed Mental Health Counselor (LMHC), and registered Clinical Supervisor with the State of Florida Board prior to her relocation. Adriana is also a Board-Certified Behavior Analyst and a Licensed Clinical Psychologist in the State of Tennessee.

KeynotesinHisPresence.org captures Adriana's life journey. She is mindful of her walk with Jesus Christ 'everywhere' she goes. She adores her Savior and Redeemer.

Email: TheBibleReadingJournalSeries@gmail.com
Subscribe to Blog: KeynotesinHisPresence.org
Join the Public Pages on Facebook:
Keynotes in His Presence & The Bible Reading Journal Series.
Join the FB closed community for women:
The Bible Reading Journal Series.

The Bible Reading Journal Series: 120 Days in the Bible.

The Bible Reading Journal Series

The Bible Reading Journal Illustrated.

The Bible Reading Journal Series: Growing Closer to God One Day at a Time.
The Bible Reading Journal Series: Rest and Be Refreshed.
The Bible Reading Journal Series: Praise and Be Content.
The Bible Reading Journal Series: Forgive and Be Restored.

The Bible Reading Journal Series: The Book of Psalms.
Special Edition.
The Bible Reading Journal Series: 120 Days in the Bible.
The Bible Reading Journal Series: Note-Taking Edition.

El Diario que te Ayudara en la Lectura de la Biblia: Cada vez mas cerca de Dios, un dia a la vez. Spanish Edition.

The Bible Reading Journal: 120 days in the Bible.
"Your Word is a lamp to my feet. And a light to my path."
Psalm 119:105

No part of this publication may be reproduced, stored in a retrieval system or transmitted in any form by any means, electronic, mechanical, photocopy, recording, or otherwise, without the prior permission of the author, except as provided for by USA copyright law.

Cover and Book design: Adriana Morales-Spokane, 2019.